Doggie
Homes

Doggie
Homes

Barkitecture for Your Best Friend

LARK BOOKS

A Division of Sterling Publishing Co., Inc.
New York

Series Editor: Dawn Cusick
Contributing Writer: Jess Clarke
Series Designer: Thom Gaines
Art Director: Thom Gaines
Cover Designer: DIY Network
Assistant Editor: Matt Paden
Art Production Assistant: Matt Paden
Editorial Assistance: Robb Helmkamp, Jesse Paden
Illustrators: Lauren Kussro, Rachel Burggraf, Charlie Covington
Photographers: Jeff Woods, Jack Parker
Photography Assistance: Gene Priest

10 9 8 7 6 5 4 3 2 1

First Edition

Published by Lark Books, A Division of
Sterling Publishing Co., Inc.
387 Park Avenue South, New York, N.Y. 10016

Text © 2006, Lark Books
Photography © 2006, DIY Network unless otherwise specified
Illustrations © 2006, DIY Network

Distributed in Canada by Sterling Publishing,
c/o Canadian Manda Group, 165 Dufferin Street
Toronto, Ontario, Canada M6K 3H6

Distributed in the United Kingdom by GMC Distribution Services,
Castle Place, 166 High Street, Lewes, East Sussex, England BN7 1XU

Distributed in Australia by Capricorn Link (Australia) Pty Ltd.,
P.O. Box 704, Windsor, NSW 2756 Australia

If you have questions or comments about this book, please contact:
Lark Books
67 Broadway
Asheville, NC 28801
(828) 253-0467

Manufactured in China

ISBN 13: 978-1-57990-853-9
ISBN 10: 1-57990-853-5

**For information about custom editions,
special sales, premium and corporate purchases,
please contact Sterling Special Sales Department
at 800-805-5489 or specialsales@sterlingpub.com.**

Contents

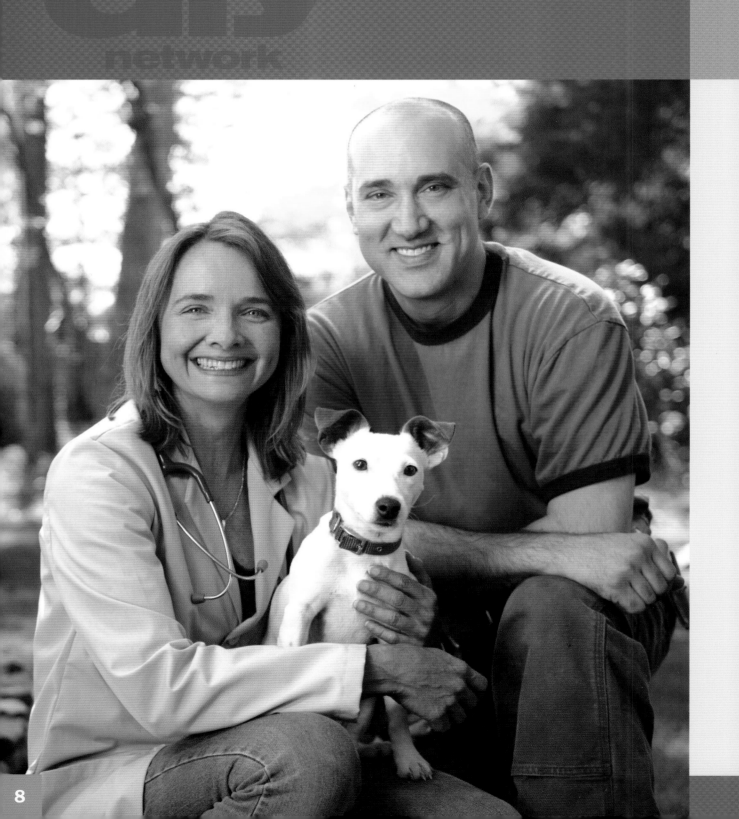

Doggie Homes

These days, when you can buy a manufactured doghouse that will address all of your pet's needs, why would you put hammer to nail to create something yourself? It's probably because you want to make a structure that's not only useful but is an adornment to your yard or house. *Barkitecture* gives you an opportunity to show your love and commitment to your dog in an inspired way. By honoring your pet, you help integrate the dog into your family. When we set out to design a pagoda for Oliver (see page 28), we wanted to craft an addition for the family's home. We ended up with a beautiful haven for Oliver and a show-piece for his human parents that all enjoy.

Your goal may be simply to create a warm and dry house for your dog, but it doesn't have to stop there. The dog's heritage can give you ideas for a style of structure. A German shepherd, for example, might lead you to a classically-styled German villa, or the proud history of an Australian cattle dog's surveying its flock may inspire you to choose a treehouse. The personality or background of your pooch might influence your design decision. With Oreo and Casey, their past had led them down different paths until they were adopted and settled in their new home. (See page 68.) Their travels provided the cues we worked from. For them, we designed and built a travel trailer, tow hitch and all.

If a doghouse is not what you're after, *Barkitecture* covers other needs, too. We built a watering trough for five thirsty English bulldogs and a dog run for two rambunctious pooches that don't have a fenced yard but love to get outside and stretch their legs. (See pages 104 and 98). You'll even find a step stool that raises three tiny Yorkies high enough off the ground to peer out the front window of their home. (See page 88.) The possibilities with *Barkitecture* are unlimited and give you options for making wonderful gifts for your pet.

Producing a television show is a challenging task, but *Barkitecture* has been a rewarding experience for everyone involved. Throughout the process, our hosts, Barkitect Kenny Alfonso and veterinarian Dr. Karen Tobias, have worked with families to help them integrate a new member into their homes. The interaction between humans and their pets is richer through the opportunity to create a house or other structure for the dog. Most episodes of the show begin by introducing the lucky dog that has been adopted from an animal shelter.

Kenny shows each family that with a little forethought and some sweat equity, building a great doghouse, a food storage cabinet, or something else for your pet can be fun and satisfying. To help families adjust to pet ownership and to inform viewers, Dr. Karen discusses topics including pet adoption, puppy-proofing your house, training a puppy, breed-specific ailments, and grooming tips and techniques. Another element of the show focuses on dog health and safety with information from Dr. Karen. We included in the book some of the best vet tips as a bonus for you and your dog.

Whether you decide to build a doghouse, a watering trough, or another structure for your dog, think of your creation as a way to welcome your pet to the family. We think you'll enjoy being a Barkitect!

Left: Dr. Karen Tobias and Kenny Alfonso,
Co-hosts of DIY's *Barkitecture*

Doggle Homes

network

1

Barkitecture Basics

Anyone can build a doghouse. To build a home for a dog, though, takes a little more work. This chapter introduces you to the basics of building one-of-a-kind doggie homes that are perfectly suited for your canine companion. None of the techniques and tips offered in this chapter is complex. They simply require you to give some forethought to your dog and his or her unique size, location, personality, and temperament. Will your dog use the home for protection from the sun or cold? Will the house be indoors or out? Is your dog prone to chewing or gnawing on everything around him or her? Does your yard slope downhill? Once you've read this chapter, you'll be ready to create your own great barkitecture!

BARKITECTURE BASICS

Everyone knows that animals make great companions. And because dogs are among the most loyal and loving pets, they deserve your care and affection, too. One way to show your love is by providing a safe, stylish, and comfortable house for your pet. Doghouses can be designed for outdoor or indoor use. A house built for the outside can help protect your pet from frostbite and intense heat, while minimizing exposure to such parasites as mites, fleas, and ticks. Indoor houses can be viewed as another piece of furniture and give your pooch a room of its own within your home. A well-built doghouse, whether it's inside or outside, helps integrate a pet into your family's life and makes it feel important. Building your own doghouse is a great opportunity for your family to act as a team and take pride in creating a classy space for your canine friend!

A doghouse can be a celebration of your pooch's ancestry and a beautiful addition to your home.

Be creative when you imagine a doghouse. Think beyond a structure that has four walls and sits on the ground. Many designs are available that depart from that concept. Depending on the dog's breed, a treehouse could be perfect, for example. Cattle dogs and other working dogs may appreciate a house where they can perch on the porch and survey the land from above the ground. A doghouse where your pet may retreat when he is inside your home may be most appropriate. A pagoda-style doghouse is such an option. By creating an indoor house from fine woods and paying attention to the detail work, you will build a haven for your pet and a beautiful addition to your family room.

◀ DESIGN DECISIONS ▶

To select a doghouse design, consider both practical and aesthetic issues. If you love to build things, you may prefer a more complex project. If your doghouse will be inside, maybe you'll want to choose a project that enhances your décor or addresses storage needs.

Consider the breed of your dog while planning his home. Some working breeds might like an elevated view like the one offered in this treehouse.

Inspiration. A dog's ancestry can influence your design decisions. (See the pagoda on page 28 that celebrates Oliver's Asian ancestry.) If your dog has German heritage, the German house or bow house might suit your pooch. If your pet will be with children a lot, consider a project the kids will especially enjoy, such as the puzzle house or schoolhouse.

Size. If you're building a doghouse for your dog to live in, size is important. The dimensions of the house should be based on the dog's size. If you live in an area with severe winters, these guidelines should be followed very closely because, in the right sized house, a dog is able to serve as his own insulation. If you live where winters are mild, you'll have more flexibility to make the house to your own specifications.

Outdoor houses can be a fun mix of practicality and style, as in this German heritage home.

The height of the house should be between 25 to 50 percent higher than the height of the dog, and the width should be the distance of your dog from nose to flank (don't count the tail in the measurement) plus 25 percent. The house's opening should be positioned about two inches lower than the dog's height. If you follow these guidelines, your dog should be able to move comfortably within his house and keep warm in winter. See the sidebar on page 64 for information on downsizing or upsizing the houses in the book.

Indoors or Out? Many family dogs, including toy breeds and some large breeds, don't live well outside. Check with a veterinarian before making a decision to house your dog outside full time.

If your pet will spend a lot of time in an outdoor doghouse, be sure to choose a design that's easy to clean. This usually requires a removable roof, which allows you to hose it out while letting it dry in the sun. Reaching through a doghouse door to clean can be awkward and inefficient.

Flat roofs. Flat roofs create problems because of their tendency to pool water. If you add just a slight angle to the roof, water will drain easily. Some dogs like to spend time on top of their houses, so a roof with less pitch may be a better choice for those pets.

BUILDING MATERIALS

Choosing the right building materials is an important part of the process. Doghouses are not covered by building codes and no one will inspect your handiwork, so it's important you make well-educated decisions that are in your dog's best interest.

Safety. Fiberglass, insulation, and other potentially toxic materials may hurt a dog if he chews or ingests them. Naturalized and rubberized materials are safer choices.

Choose weather-resistant materials for outdoor homes, such as the composite decking material in this shade house.

Durability. Select materials that will withstand the elements if the house will be outdoors. Choose outdoor-rated materials, including pressure-treated lumber, so the structure will last.

Outdoor-graded paints are safe for dogs. For outside houses, check the manufacturer's labels to be sure the paint offers UV (ultraviolet) protection.

If you're considering building an ornate structure, remember that your dog may chew or eat any little pieces attached to the house, potentially causing damage to both your dog and his house.

Comfort. Bedding materials are an important decision, also. Commercially manufactured bedding is often weather resistant and can be a good choice. Even old blankets or towels may be perfect, as long as they can be washed weekly to limit flea and tick populations and reduce smell.

For a natural alternative, cedar chips work well because they help repel mites and other parasites. Avoid using hay, which can harbor parasites, insects, molds, fungi, and dust.

If you plan to insulate the doghouse, make sure the insulation is not exposed and that your dog can't get to it. Try using a non-toxic insulation foam sheet that can be sandwiched between the walls of the house.

Some people choose to outfit their doghouse with air conditioning and heat, which, in severe climates, can be helpful. Freestanding electric units are made specifically for doghouses.

Make sure your dog's new space is comfortable. Supply bedding material, towels or, cedar chips for it to lie on.

Fun accessories like windows can also be practical additions to your dog's home.

ACCESSORIES

There's nothing wrong with a simple, attractive, and functional doghouse, but there are lots of ways you can increase the whimsy and/or practicality of your dog's home.

Lights & Music. It's fairly simple to wire a doghouse for lights and/or music, although this is probably more for your entertainment than for your dog's.

Natural Light. Windows can give your dog light and a view of his territory. In some cases, you can make a window by cutting a hole in the house, framing it with wood, and cutting glass or clear plastic sheeting to fit the opening. Demo windows, to add a decorator's touch, are sometimes available from window companies.

Doors. In areas with lots of wind, rain, or cold weather, a dog door can be useful. Make sure the door is removable for summer months.

Safety Note: Some dog doors seal so well that they can make a home airtight, which may lead to suffocation. To prevent this problem, cut several ventilation holes near the roofline.

BUILDING TIMES

Each project in the book features a page that provides additional information about special features and design considerations. You'll also find a note about the time needed to finish the project. These times are estimates for a builder with average skills. The time you need to complete a project may differ from our estimate.

When considering estimated building times, it's important to remember that more hours don't always reflect a project's level of difficulty. The log cabin, for example, may appear to be a time-intensive project. The building of the house, though, just requires careful measuring, cutting, and assembling. The steps are repetitive but not diffficult for the average builder.

CHOOSING A SITE

Outdoor Houses. As with most real estate, location is very important. Look for a location that gets as much direct sunlight as possible during winter months. The site should be away from mud and running water. Be sure to position the opening or door of the house to minimize exposure to the elements. This can be as simple as making the opening face downhill, not uphill, if there's a grade to the land to prevent water from running into the structure.

You might want to consider changing site locations when the seasons change. In the summer, you can make the house more livable by moving it to a shaded location or putting a tarp over the structure.

If you can't avoid dirt and mud, place the house on bricks or concrete blocks to minimize moisture and mold damage. Keep the bedding dry, too.

Indoor Houses. Doghouses inside create a private space for dogs, their own retreat. And because they're not exposed to the elements, inside houses offer an opportunity to make the structure part of your home décor. If it's built well, an interior house can be a piece of fine, handcrafted furniture.

Maintenance and cleaning are important for indoor and outdoor houses. Be on the lookout for worn out or frayed materials and other unsafe items your dog might like to eat.

If you want to showcase the house as furniture, consider its location the way you would with any other piece of furniture. If you think your dog needs the house as a retreat, choose a quiet corner.

TIPS DIY Network Home Improvement

SPECIAL-NEEDS DOGS

For dogs with medical conditions, houses may need special design considerations. A dog with vision problems, for example, would do best with a structure with rounded corners and padding inside. Dogs with bone and joint problems might appreciate a low entrance hole or a small step stool.

Choose house sites that are warm during the winter. Use pavers or bricks to reduce the amount of mud in and around the site.

◣ MAINTENANCE ◢

Maintenance is important for both your dog's health and for the doghouse, especially outdoor doghouses.

Routine Home Inspections. Dogs bite and chew, so clean up any frayed or chewed materials. Look for exposed nail tips that could cut your dog's skin or get caught in its collar. Be sure to inspect the house occasionally. If the structure has insulation, check the house more frequently to minimize the chance your dog will ingest it. For doghouses without flat roofs, examine the inside of the roof structure for wasp and hornet nests.

Dog runs provide a safe place for dogs to run and play. See page 98 for ways to make the run odor free.

Cleaning. Outdoor doghouses should be washed and thoroughly hosed out as often as your dog's behavior and routines require. Allow the interior of the house to completely dry before replacing bedding materials. Bedding should be removed and cleaned or replaced as needed to prevent mold and ensure good insulation.

SCALE: ENLARGING AND REDUCING

There are many ways to change the scale, or size, of an object. Some scales and grid systems are fairly easy to use, and others are more challenging. Whether changing the size of a house or a piece of furniture, you use the same basic processes to reduce or enlarge the object.

One of the easiest ways to change the scale of an object is with an architect's scale. This three-sided, foot-long ruler has 11 scale ratios that range from 12 inches equals 1 foot (1:1) to $\frac{3}{32}$ of an inch equals 1 foot (1:128). The implement is used to draw and design buildings, furniture, and other mechanical objects at a specific proportion and scale. You can buy a scale from your local drafting supplier or arts and crafts store, or use a regular ruler to create a makeshift scale.

To change scale with an architect's scale, first determine the full scale (1:1) measurements of the object you need to reduce or enlarge. Then draw the object using a smaller scale so you can fit it on the paper you're using. This scale gradation may be $\frac{3}{16}$" equals 1' (1:64) or another similar smaller scale such as $\frac{1}{8}$" equals 1' (1:96). Typically, the size of the paper you use will determine the scale you'll use to draw the object. The smaller the paper, the smaller the scale and vice versa.

Q&A WITH DR. KAREN TOBIAS

VETERINARY TIPS FOR BUILDING DOGHOUSES

Building a great doghouse is about more than just cutting wood and hammering nails—your design should create a clean, safe, and comfortable environment your dog will want to call home. Here, Dr. Karen shares her advice on how to make a doghouse your veterinarian would be proud of.

Q: HOW DO I GET MY DOG TO USE A DOGHOUSE?

A: No matter how much effort you put into building your pet a house, your dog may be hesitant or even unwilling to use it. Remember that the doghouse is there to provide shelter and security; not every dog needs a doghouse to obtain such comforts. A dog should associate its new house with positive experiences and should never be forced inside. Give your pup plenty of time to get used to the doghouse, and encourage exploration by putting favorite toys, bedding, or treats inside. A dog should consider his new digs to be a special retreat, so the doghouse should never be used as a place for punishment. And, let the children know that the doghouse is your pet's private space—even pooches need to get away once in a while.

Q: WHAT ARE THE BASIC REQUIREMENTS OF AN OUTDOOR DOGHOUSE?

A: Outdoor doghouses should protect your pets from the elements—particularly wind, rain, and sun— and should be small enough so that the dog can warm it with its own body heat. Additionally, they should be well-ventilated to prevent moisture build up and improve air circulation, since poorly ventilated, high humidity environments can increase the risk of allergies and infections from mold, mildew, viruses, and bacteria.

Q: HOW SHOULD I WEATHERPROOF THE HOUSE?

A: Dogs don't need a lot of insulation in their houses, since their fur coats provide them with protection from the cold. In fact, extra insulation can trap moisture within the doghouse and can be life threatening if eaten. If you live in a really cold climate, consider a double-walled structure so that the pocket of air trapped between the two walls can act as an insulating barrier without inhibiting air or moisture flow. Ventilation holes or a louvered window can be added near the roof peak or under the eaves to improve air circulation.

In warm climates, consider elevating the doghouse several inches to improve air circulation under and around the structure. In cold climates, a "skirt" or wind block can be added around the base of an elevated house to improve insulation, and a swinging door can be added over the doorway to keep out drafts. Many dogs enjoy chewing carpet and canvas, so make sure to take into consideration your dog's disposition when choosing materials for doorway barriers. Doorways can be offset—cut nearer to the corner of the house—to reduce exposure to weather extremes.

Q: WHAT IS THE BEST LOCATION FOR AN OUTDOOR DOGHOUSE?

A: Choose a site that is protected from severe weather. For example, the door should face away from prevailing winds in the winter, and house itself can be placed away from the path of any storm. For example, in our area, storms often come from the west, so dog houses are more sheltered on the Eastern side of the house. Additionally, make sure that the house is in full shade in the summer in cool climates and year round in warmer climates so that your dog

DIY co-host and veterinarian Dr. Karen Tobias

doesn't become overheated. Dog houses placed near fences and garden walls become stair steps to freedom for escape artists, so consider placing houses away from them.

Q: ARE THERE ANY SPECIAL RECOMMENDATIONS FOR INDOOR HOUSES?

A: Indoor houses should be easily cleanable, so a removable roof is a must if one is added at all. Consider making a doghouse that either comes apart or fits through doorways easily so it can be moved. Large doghouses can be placed on castors or rollers to improve mobility as long as these can be locked in place. Use lightweight materials that are durable and easy to clean.

Doggle Homes

2

Doghouses

A purely functional, perfectly respectable doghouse can be found in stores everywhere. Doghouses with an architectural flair, though—barkitecture—are special treasures. This chapter features a range of dog homes in styles and shapes that are as unique as your pet. All of the homes can be adapted to suit the size and personality of your dog and your home's décor. From an Oriental palace to a log cabin, from a treehouse to a replica of your own house, this chapter will help you choose and build just the right home for your canine companion.

HOME SWEET HOME

This fun-shaped house is designed for a smaller house dog who enjoys sleeping with the kids. The roof is embellished with cutout shapes that can be customized to suit the dog, the season, or your child's room décor.

◣ PROJECT SUMMARY ◢

The house is just as fun to build as it will be for Tess to sleep in and the family to look at. The house is made from Baltic birch plywood with exaggerated angles for a cartoonish effect and is built without screws or nails. It's really just one big puzzle!

You Will Need

- 2 4' x 8' sheets of ½" birch plywood
- 1 4' x 8' sheet of ¼" plywood
- Sawhorses
- Wood file
- Safety glasses
- Ear protection
- Tape measure
- Plunge router with ½" straight bit and ¼" roundover bit
- 2 bar clamps
- 4' level or straightedge
- Wood stain
- Polyurethane
- Shop towels
- Jigsaw
- Random orbit sander with 150 grit pads

PUZZLE
STEP BY STEP

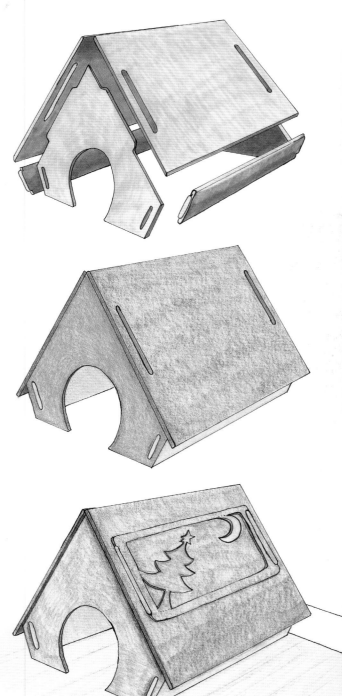

1 Start by crosscutting (cutting against the grain) both of the ½" sheets of birch plywood to make four 48 x 48 pieces. Use the level or a straightedge to make a line connecting marks you've made 48" from the corners of one end. Clamp the level to the wood to provide a guide for the circular saw to follow. Once the base of the saw is against the guide, make sure the blade is on the line, then start cutting.

2 Rip (or cut with the grain) two 12" pieces —one each from two of the 48 x 48 pieces— to make the side walls. Label and set them aside for now.

FIGURE A: Side wall template

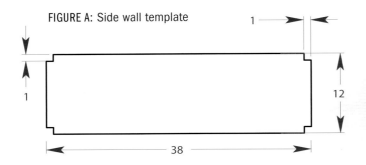

1

1

12

38

TESS PLAYS WITH HER PUZZLE

DESIGN DECISIONS

Tess will spend a lot of time inside, especially in a young boy's room. A puzzle-style dog-house is just right for the set-ting. Exaggerated angles give the structure a cartoonish effect. Nails and screws are not used because the house pieces fit together like a puzzle. And that's safer for a child's room.

MAKING A HOUSE A HOME

Building tip: A router is useful in woodworking. Hold it tightly and move it smoothly, so it doesn't get away from you.

Estimated building time: 6–8 hours

A DOG'S LIFE

To help children keep up with the needs of a new pet, create a schedule for them to follow daily.

A FRIENDLY BONE TO PICK

Give your dog healthy snacks that are tasty and less fattening. You can find organic snacks and treats for special needs of canines. Treats with meat as the main ingredient are good to use. If you make the snacks yourself, you know your pet is eating healthy food.

DOG TALES

▬ The average lifespan of a dog is 10 to 15 years. Keep that in mind when deciding about getting a dog.

▬ The Humane Society of the United States recommends not giving an adopted pet as a gift at holidays. Unwanted animals often return to shelters.

3 The two pieces left after cutting the sidewalls should measure 36 x 48. These will be the front and rear gabled walls. Start laying out the first wall by finding the centerline of the sheet. Find the center point of the 36" edges by measuring in 18" from each corner, then connect the two points with the straightedge (photo A).

4 Determine which edge will be the base of the wall. Measure up 36" from the base along the centerline and make a mark. This will be the peak of the roof. From the center point of the base, measure 13" along the edge and make a mark. Measure up 9½" from the corner, make a mark, then connect the two points. This line should measure 10¾". Repeat these steps for the corner on the opposite side of the centerline. Now connect the ends of these lines to the peak marked on the centerline. These lines should measure 32" when finished.

5 Next, lay out the tenons, or tabs, that will attach the roof panels. The tenons are 16" long and 1" wide, and should be centered on the edges that will connect to the roof. Use a jigsaw to cut the outline of the first wall, then use it as a template to trace the second wall.

FIGURE B: Front wall template

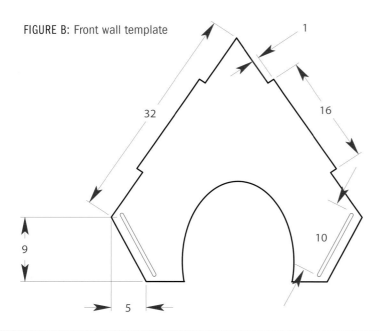

NUTRITION

Vitamins are a type of nutritional supplement, and not all dogs need them. Vitamins are very important to use if your dog is on a vegetarian diet, or a homemade diet. They will help make the diet complete and balanced.

One type of nutritional supplement is a glucosamine-chondroitin sulfate. These medications are used particularly for dogs that have joint problems. Dogs with arthritis get a lot of swelling and inflammation inside their joints, and the nutraceuticals have been shown to reduce inflammation and slow down the progression of joint disease.

Another supplement is fatty acids. Essential fatty acids are found in flax oil, sunflower oil and fish oils. They reduce the amounts of inflammation in different parts of the body, including the skin. They are often recommended by veterinarians for animals that have itchy skin or dry hair coat, or are also on an unbalanced diet.

Some nutraceuticals are used in dogs that have liver disease. You want to make sure that if you use nutraceuticals you have the recommendation of your veterinarian. They are not safe for all pets. One important thing to know about all of these medications is that they are not regulated by the government, and therefore you can't be absolutely sure about the content.

6 Lay out and cut the mortises, or slots, in the front and rear walls that accept the tenons of the side walls. The mortises will be ½" wide, 10" long, and run parallel to the wall edges 1¼" away. The ends of the mortise should be 1" from the roof edge and the base edge. To make the cut, use the plunge router with a ½" straight bit (photo F). Use a straight-edged guide as with the saws.

7 Set the front and rear walls aside, and locate the sidewalls previously cut. Crosscut them to a length of 38", then lay out and cut 1 x 10 tenons centered on both ends of the walls (photo G).

8 Make two roof panels from the remaining 48 x 48 sheets of plywood. Rip to a width of 35" and crosscut at 39½". Layout mortises on the roof panels that are 16" long and 1¼" away from the front and rear edges. They should start 8" away from the top edge and end 11" away from the bottom edge.

9 With a wood file, round the square ends of all tenons so that they fit into the mortises.

10 Cut a hole in the front wall for a door. To get a symmetrical, rounded opening, make a template with a sheet of paper folded in half and cut to size. Unfold the paper, trace this form, and follow this line with the jigsaw.

11 With the ¼" roundover bit in the router, ease the edges of the door and roof as well as wall edges that touch the floor.

12 Sand and finish the panels. Use a random orbital sander with 150 grit pads to sand all surfaces. Then apply stain and polyurethane following the directions provided on the label. Let the parts dry completely, then assemble them.

FIGURE C: Roof panel template

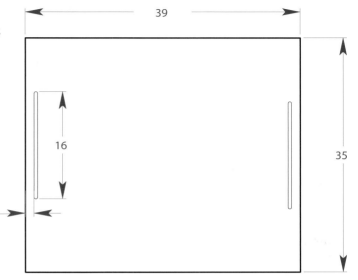

13 Use a jigsaw with a detail-cutting blade to cut seasonal designs from the ¼" plywood (photo H). These stencils will sit on the exposed tabs, so leave ½" of overhang on the top wall of the stencil frame.

PAGODA PALACE

This classy house, built to be indoors, adds an Asian flair to your home. The nice wood and trimming make it a piece of furniture. It's a beautiful choice whether your dog's ancestry is Irish, English, Asian, or something else.

◀ PROJECT SUMMARY ▶

The pagoda only looks difficult to build. The basic frame consists of a box made of white oak plywood that will be decorated to give it a pagoda feel. The element that makes this more than just a doghouse is the roof structure, with the traditional sloping lines of a pagoda.

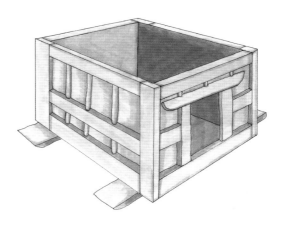

PAGODA STEP BY STEP

You Will Need

- 1 sheet of ⅛" pressboard
- Walnut trim
- 1 sheet of ⅛" white oak plywood
- Poplar trim
- Bag of architectural roof tiles
- Tung oil
- Safety glasses
- Tape measure
- Pencil

- Table saw
- Electric drill
- Screws
- Chop saw
- Pocket hole jig
- Jigsaw
- Pneumatic brad-nailer
- Small and medium spring clamps
- Air compressor

1 Cut the plywood walls to the desired dimensions. Our example is:
- 2 pieces 18 x 16 for the front and back walls
- 2 pieces 18 x 24 for the side walls
- 4 pieces 1 x 1 x 18-long corner cleats

2 To get the box shape of the doghouse, cut out the door at 9 x 14. Assemble the walls (photo A) with corner cleats using a pneumatic brad-nailer. Nail through the face of the walls into the cleats. The nails will be covered by the decorative trim you'll add.

A

FINE-LIVING ZEN

DESIGN DECISIONS

Pugs originated in China, so a pagoda is a perfect palace for Oliver, a pug mix. He will spend most of his time inside, an opportunity to create a structure with wood and trim to complement the home's decor. The roof comes off for easy cleaning. Enjoy the conversation piece.

MAKING A HOUSE A HOME

Building tip: The pocket hole jig you'll use is available at any home-improvement store. The tool comes with a modified clamp and square-head screws. The drill bit's collar gives more control over drilling depth.

Estimated building time: 12–14 hours

A DOG'S LIFE

Pugs can have breathing problems, so it may be best to use a harness that won't stress their windpipe if they pull. It's normal for pugs to breathe and snore loudly.

A FRIENDLY BONE TO PICK

Leather and nylon leashes work well. It's important to get a leash that's the right size for your dog, a leash that's short enough to give you control but long enough for him to reach the grass.

DOG TALES

In 1785, a dog became the first living being to use a parachute when French inventor J.P. Blanchard dropped a canine from a hot-air balloon.

3 Cut the decorative walnut-trim pieces to these dimensions (photo B):

- raw stock 1½ x ¾
- 8 pieces 18" long (for sides)
- 6 pieces 15" long (for sides)
- 5 pieces 13" long (for the back)
- 2 pieces 14" long (for the door's side trim)
- 1 piece 12" long (for over the door)
- raw stock ½ x ½
- 6 pieces 9½" long
- 6 pieces 4" long

4 The frame's dimensions are 18 x 24 with a horizontal strut 4" up from the top of the bottom rail (photo C). With the brad-nailer, attach the trim pieces. The outer frame is constructed with the pocket hole jig. The jig can be bought from a home store and comes with the drill bit, specialized clamp and jig that make seamless joints.

5 Cut the ½" walnut-trim pieces to fit within the frame that is made from the 1½" pieces (photo D).

6 Cut the roof components, two at 1½ x 18 long.

7 Trace the shape of the trusses. The roof's curved slope can be drawn with any round object, such as a trash can lid or flying disc (photo E).

DENTAL HYGIENE

Did you know that dogs get dental disease just like people do? In fact, dogs that have a lot of plaque and tartar can actually have more problems with kidney and heart disease. So, it is important for you to take care of their teeth. You have several different options.

You can use dental wipes to rub the outside surface of the teeth and get the plaque off.

You can use a toothbrush that is made specifically for dogs. You can use it to slide along the outside surfaces of your dog's teeth. If you want to use toothpaste, choose one that is made specifically for dogs. Dogs will swallow toothpaste, so you don't want to give them anything with fluoride.

If you can't get to your dog's teeth every day, you can provide them with dental chews. As the dog chews, it will break off the tartar and plaque.

Toys can help, too. Some fit in and around the teeth, and that also breaks down tartar and plaque.

You can use a dental rinse. Some of the rinses are only to improve your dog's breath, but others actually have antibacterials in them to kill the bacteria that cause plaque.

8 Cut out two roof trusses from the ¾" walnut board. Attach the shaped pieces to the horizontals with the pin-nailer. Attach the ridge beam (½ x ½) to the top of the trusses (photo F).

TIPS DIY Network Home Improvement

KERFING

Although it may sound like something your dog would do on the carpet, kerfing is really a woodworking technique. It may sound strange, but the result is pretty neat. Kerfs are grooves cut into a piece of wood with a saw at regularly spaced intervals. The purpose of these grooves is to reduce the thickness of the wood, allowing it to become more flexible. Once a piece of wood has been kerfed, it can bend and mold more readily to fit the contours of a curved surface, like the roof of our pagoda.

9 Cut two pieces of pressboard at 25 x 16. Set the table saw blade to $\frac{1}{16}$" to cut kerfs in the pressboard. Cut the relief cuts along the long dimensions of the pressboard at $\frac{1}{8}$" intervals (photo G).

10 Attach the pressboard to the roof trusses with $\frac{1}{2}$" #6 wood screws (pre-drill to avoid splitting). Then attach the roof tiles with silicone (photo H). Finish with tung oil as desired.

COPPER'S CABIN

For any doghouse, it's a good idea to consider the dog's size and personality and the location and setting of your home. A log cabin might be just the house if you're in a wooded area with wildflowers. But the house is a cozy and rugged addition to any setting. And you can get inside to clean it!

◀ PROJECT SUMMARY ▶

The doghouse should be big enough to allow your pet to turn around inside but small enough to retain his body heat. You'll need landscaping timbers, lap joints for each corner and, for the foundation, nice stone pavers. You'll finish it off with a removable standing metal roof.

You Will Need

- 18 landscape timbers, 8' long
- 12 concrete pavers
- Two 2 x 4s, 8' long
- Two 2 x 2s, 8' long
- One ½" sheet of 4 x 8 plywood
- Special-order standing seam metal roof
- Sand
- Safety glasses
- Tape measure
- Pencil
- Table saw
- Radial arm saw
- T-stands
- Level
- Hammer
- Wood chisel
- Construction adhesive
- Caulk gun
- Electric drill
- Screws
- Chinking caulk
- Angle square

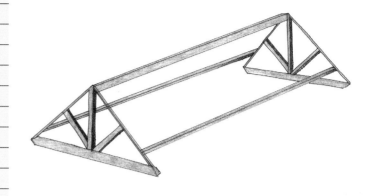

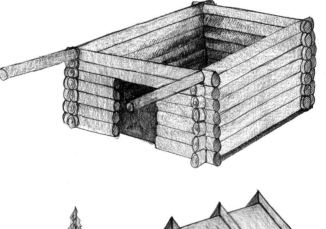

1 Cut all timbers as follows:
- 32 pieces 42" long
- 20 pieces 14" long
- 2 pieces 60" long

2 Rip all timbers to 3" wide. Set the table saw or radial saw to 3" wide, and run all timbers through (photo A). This matches them in size and fits them more easily together later.

A

RUSTIC CHARM

DESIGN DECISIONS

Factors that influence the design of Copper's doghouse include his size and personality and the setting of the family's home. It's also important that the family can get inside Copper's cabin to clean it. With a fenced garden, wildflowers and woods behind the house, the rustic and natural log cabin style fits well.

At 28" x 40", the cabin's cozy interior accommodates Copper's dimensions with a few inches to spare. The roof may be removed to clean the house.

MAKING A HOUSE A HOME

Estimated building time: 16–18 hours

A DOG'S LIFE

Golden retrievers make great family dogs because they're very social. With a thick undercoat and a topcoat, they need weekly brushing. The dogs like to eat, so it's a good idea to portion their food with a measuring cup—15 to 18 ounces a day—and monitor treats.

A FRIENDLY BONE TO PICK

In addition to collars and tattoos, microchipping is a way to identify your dog. The chip, the size of a grain of rice, is inserted in the dog's skin. A rescue agency can scan the top of the microchip and get a computerized number. With a phone call, the agency will have information about you and your pet to reunite you.

DOG TALES

▬ After the Labrador retriever, the golden retriever is the second most popular canine breed in the United States. About 60,000 goldens are registered nationally.

▬ Golden retrievers, known for their pleasant temperament, are used in search-and-rescue missions and as guide dogs for the blind and therapy dogs for the elderly.

3 Next, cut the notches out of the timbers. Set the radial arm saw to $1\frac{1}{4}$" deep. On the 42" pieces, slice at $\frac{1}{4}$" increments 3" from each end to create a notch 3" wide (photo B). Clean the bottom of the cut with the wood chisel.

4 Then create notches 3" from one end on 10 of the 14" pieces, which will be used around the door. Flip and cut the remaining 10 pieces of 14" timber, and notch the opposite end.

5 Level the site at 72 x 48 then sand the entire area with about 1" of sand. The last step of the foundation is to lay the pavers (photo C). Be sure there is a slight slope toward the door or front of the doghouse for proper water drainage.

6 After the foundation is finished, begin placing the logs one level at a time. Use construction adhesive between each level by placing a bead along the length of the timbers (photo D). Repeat the process all the way to the top. Don't forget that the 14" pieces make up the dog door in the front of the cabin.

7 The materials for the roof include 1 x 1 wood, 2 x 4s and ½" plywood. The angle of the gables is your choice and will be dictated by the slope of the roof you design (photo E).

8 After the roof is assembled, you may skin as desired. Use standard roofing shingles or standing seam aluminum panels, which can be ordered to your specifications from a roofing company.

9 After the roof is assembled and skinned, place it on top of the cabin (photo F).

10 Caulk between every seam around the entire house with a caulking gun and chinking caulk (photo G).

TIPS | DIY Network Home Improvement

DADO BLADES

Decrease the amount of cutting time required to notch the landscaping timbers with a dado blade set for the radial arm saw. The blades can be stacked together to form a wider cutting blade. By covering more surface area, dado blades can remove more material with each pass of the saw, saving a lot of time in projects with many repetitive cuts.

DOGGIE SCHOOLHOUSE

Give the kids an education in building a dog-house—with a schoolhouse theme. The design, inspired by the classic little red schoolhouse image, adds a history lesson to the experience.

◣ **PROJECT SUMMARY** ◢

The design of the schoolhouse is simple, so children can help with measuring and marking. After you make the cuts, kids can help assemble the structure. You'll attach the felt-covered panels to the frame with a nail gun and attach the chalkboard top the same way. When it's finished, the kids will enjoy decorating the felt sides of the house and writing on the roof.

SCHOOLHOUSE STEP BY STEP

You Will Need

- Five pieces of 2 x 4 material, 8' long
- Two 4 x 8 sheets of ⅛" plywood
- Two pieces of half-round decorative molding, 8' long
- Wood screws
- Felt, a variety of colors
- Colored chalk
- Chalkboard paint
- Safety glasses
- Tape measure
- Square
- Table saw
- Chop saw
- Pneumatic nail gun
- Paintbrushes
- Staple gun
- Scissors
- Cordless Drill

◼ MAKING THE SCHOOLHOUSE ◼

1 Rip in half 2 x 4 material for the pieces needed to frame the house. Cut 2 x 2 or 2 x 3 stock into the following lengths: four at 30" for the sidewalls of the frame; eight at 21" (four will be used for corner posts, and four will be stretchers at the front and rear of the house); four at 13" long for the gables; and two at 27" long for the stretchers between the gables (photo A).

A

GINGER'S SCHOOLHOUSE

DESIGN DECISIONS

There's no better doghouse than a schoolhouse for a dog that hangs out in a classroom with kids or for a dog whose kids enjoy playing school. The classic little red schoolhouse is the model for this fun structure. The walls are made of felt, so kids can decorate them easily. And chalkboard paint on the roof makes the top into a chalkboard.

MAKING A HOUSE A HOME

Estimated building time: 6–8 hours

A DOG'S LIFE

Dogs talk with their bodies, so learn to read their body language. If the tale is between the legs, and the head is low, the dog probably is sad or scared. A dog with ears and tail straight up is angry. If the animal is showing its teeth, look out —it may want to bite. If you pet a dog, pet and stroke its back calmly. Petting the head can upset a dog.

A FRIENDLY BONE TO PICK

Every dog can produce dander, which causes allergies in some people. Because dog baths do a good job of removing dander, many people are tempted to over-bathe their dog. Ironically, this irritates a dog's skin and causes even more dander. Between baths, wipe off your dog with a moist cloth.

DOG TALES

The world's oldest dog lived for more than 29 years. The average lifespan for dogs is 10 to 12 years, depending on the breed and individual dog.

2 With screws, assemble the bottom and top frames, and then attach the corner posts between the two frames to bring it all together. Attach mitered parts at the front for the gables, and complete the frame by attaching stretcher rails between the gables.

3 Measure and cut ⅛" plywood for the sides, front, back, and roof (photo B). Cut two pieces at 24 x 30 for the sides. Measure for the front and back then cut. Measure for the roof and cut.

4 After all the pieces are cut out, attach the plywood panels to the frame with finish nails (photo C). Then cut out the desired door in the front panel.

5 Repeat steps 1 through 4 at one-third scale for the steeple assembly. Omit the bottom frame, and trace the front and back panels to fit over the roof.

6 Paint the roof with chalkboard paint (photo D). Measure and attach the molding at corners and around the door. For the rest of the walls, front and rear, attach the felt. Now your new doghouse is ready to decorate.

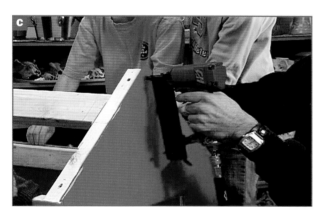

HERITAGE HOME

If you have German shepherds or other German breeds, this house can double as a heritage home, celebrating German architecture with its stucco walls, wood trim, and a pointed, round tower.

◣ **PROJECT SUMMARY** ◢

Building the heritage home starts from the ground up, beginning with the large floor area. The tower, made from a concrete form, fits in the middle of an "L" shape that you'll notch. Atop this tower sits a metal roof that you can either build yourself or order from a metal fabricator. Building this house is a three-part project. You'll measure and cut the materials, assemble them, and then finish by applying the exterior decorations.

You Will Need

- A 5 x 5 sheet of furniture-grade ¾" plywood
- Four 4 x 8 sheets of furniture-grade ¾" plywood
- Six 1 x 1½" pieces of finish-grade pine, 8' long
- Shingles
- Paint (two contrasting colors)
- 1¼" wood screws
- Concrete form 24" in diameter and at least 43" long
- Caulk
- Metal roof from metal fabricator
- Safety glasses
- Circular saw
- Jigsaw with metal-cutting blade
- Laser pointer
- Staple gun
- Paintbrushes
- Screw gun
- Countersink bit
- Pencil
- Large compass
- Tape measure
- Level
- 4' straightedge
- Caulk gun

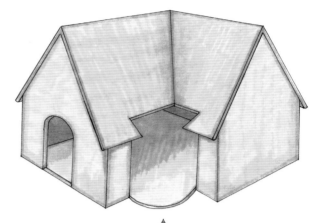

FLOOR CUTTING

1 Cut the 60 x 60 piece of ¾" plywood to 54⅜ x 54⅜ square. As in all projects, be sure to wear your safety glasses while cutting the materials.

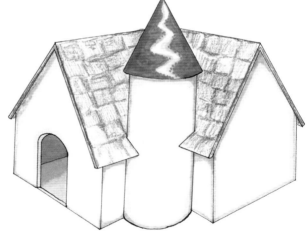

AUTHENTIC STYLING

DESIGN DECISIONS

A German-style house is perfect for two German shepherds. To get the look of stucco, you'll paint the walls. Wood trim around the side and a shingled roof will give the feel of a chalet. A rounded tower will complete the theme. The house is big, almost 5' square. For a smaller breed or just one dog, make a smaller structure. The dog must fit through the door standing up and be able to turn around inside.

MAKING A HOUSE A HOME

Building tips: Use a fine-tooth blade to cut the cylinder for the tower. Blades designed for metal-cutting work well. Coarse woodcutting blades don't give the best results.

Estimated building time: 20–24 hours

A DOG'S LIFE

To make a bed for your puppy, use something soft and washable for the dog to sleep on. If your pup seems lonely, give him something to snuggle with. Fill a bottle with warm water, wrap it in a towel, and put it in the puppy's bed.

A FRIENDLY BONE TO PICK

Puppies are especially susceptible to parasites. Some mites live on the skin and cause itching. See your veterinarian for medication.

DOG TALES

German shepherds love being with their families and are very protective. They must be extensively socialized to avoid over-guarding.

FIGURE A: Floor template

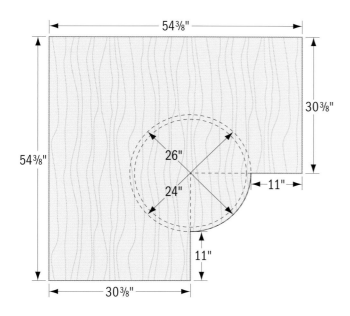

2 Measure 30⅜" from one corner, and make a mark.

3 Measure 30⅜" from the corner diagonal from the first corner, along the side perpendicular to the side where you made the first mark.

4 Measure in 11" from these marks and make a mark, and make a second mark at 24" in. The second marks from each side should intersect each other. Use this point as the center, and draw a circle 26" in diameter. The circle should intersect the marks made at 11".

5 Draw a line from each of your original marks at 30⅜" to the 11" mark where they intersect the circle.

6 Cut along each of these lines with the jigsaw. Then cut along the circle between the two previous cuts.

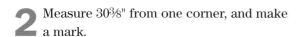 **GABLED WALL CUTTING**

7 Cut two ¾" sheets of the furniture-grade plywood to 30⅜ x 45½ (photo A).

8 Along both 45½" sides, make a mark at 22⅜" for one end.

9 Make a mark at the center of each of the 30⅜" sides by measuring 15³⁄₁₆" on the side.

10 Draw a line from each of the 22⅜" marks to the center point at the opposite end. Cut along this line to form the gable (photo B).

FIGURE B: Walls and Door

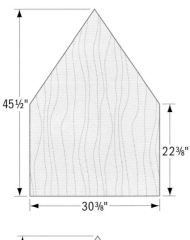

FIGURE C: Angles for front roof

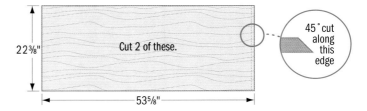

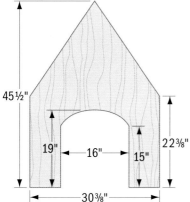

DOOR CUTTING

11 On one of the gable ends, draw and cut the door by measuring 8" in each direction along the edge, and make a mark.

12 From each of these marks, draw a line up 15" to mark the sides of the door opening.

13 From the same center mark, measure up 19" to mark the center of the top of the door.

14 Draw an arched line that connects the end of these lines with the mark at 19". Cut along the lines (photo C).

BACK WALL CUTTING

15 Cut two sheets of ¾" plywood to 23 x 55. Miter one 23" side of each at 45° to form the back corner.

FRONT WALL CUTTING

16 Cut two sheets of ¾" plywood to 23 x 11. Miter one 11" side of each at 53°.

FRONT ROOF CUTTING

17 Cut two sheets of ¾" plywood to 40¼ x 33. Along one long side, measure 11½" from the edge. Draw a line up 4½". From the end of this line, draw a line parallel to the edge across to the opposite side, ending 4½" from the corner. Cut along these lines (photo D).

18 Make a mark 25" from the 33" side along the edge of the cut you just made.

19 Draw a line diagonally from this point to the upper corner. Cut along this line at 33½° to create an inside miter.

FIGURE D: Angles for back roof

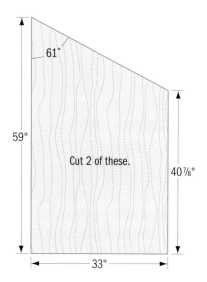

61°

59"

Cut 2 of these.

40⅞"

33"

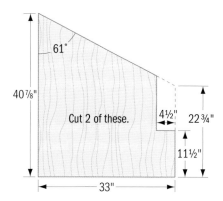

61°

40⅞"

Cut 2 of these.

4½"

22¾"

11½"

33"

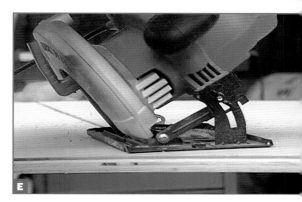

20 On each sheet, miter one of the long sides at 26° on the opposite side from the inside miter (photo E).

21 Cut two sheets of ¾" plywood to 59 x 34. Miter the 59" side at 26°.

22 On the opposite edge, measure 40¼" and make a mark.

23 From this mark, draw a line to the opposite corner.

24 Cut along this line at 33½° to create an outside miter (photo F).

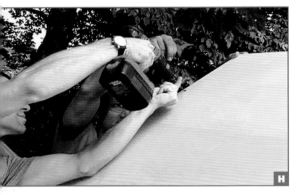

ASSEMBLY

1 Attach one gabled wall to the floor with 1¼" wood screws. Drive the screws up through the floor into the bottom edge of the gabled wall.

2 Countersink all screws flush with the wood surface.

3 Attach one of the front walls to the gabled wall by screwing through the front wall into the edge of the gabled wall and into the edge of the floor (photo G).

4 Repeat for the second gabled wall and the front wall.

5 Attach the back walls by screwing through the back wall into the edge of the floor and gabled wall. Screw the back walls together at the mitered rear corner.

6 Level and attach the back roof panels by screwing them to the edge of the back and gabled walls (photo H).

ATTACHING THE CYLINDER

7 Cut the 24"-diameter cylinder to 43" long with the jigsaw fitted with a metal-cutting blade.

8 Set the cylinder in place to touch both front walls (photo I).

9 Mount a laser pointer to a piece of ¾" material (photo J), so when it is slid along the surface of the gabled walls and the back roof sections, it will project a point where the front roof panels will intersect the cylinder. Mark the cylinder where the laser hits the cylinder every inch or so. Then connect these points. Cut along this line with the jigsaw.

10 Attach the front roof sections (photo K). To help align the roof panels, add a strip of wood to the inside of each panel where they contact the walls. This will support the weight of the panels and ensure a good fit.

11 Set the cylinder in place (photo L). Screw through the cylinder into the roof and walls to attach it.

12 Caulk all the seams, then paint the house as desired.

13 Shingle the wood roof according to the manufacturer's instructions (photo M).

◢ EXTERIOR DECORATION ◣

1 Cut 1½ x 1 material to size and taste. Attach the material with finish nails (photo N).

2 Paint the material a contrasting color to set it off from the rest of the house, and your dog's heritage home is complete.

TIPS | DIY Network Home Improvement

SHINGLING

One way to increase the weatherproofing on your dog's house is to add roofing felt before laying the shingles. Roofing felt and shingles work well together; the felt provides a great waterproofing layer while the shingles protect the felt and the plywood roof from harsh weather conditions. Roofing felt can be bought in rolls, and is easily applied with roofing nails.

MADE IN THE SHADE

Overheating is as dangerous for dogs as it is for people. This shade structure will help keep your dog cool and content, especially if your yard has no trees or other shade.

◀ PROJECT SUMMARY ▶

The house without walls will provide lots of shade and still allow air to circulate through it. Durability is important because the structure will be left outside year-round in the elements. The sturdy composite material you'll use doesn't need weatherproofing or paint. Choose a fabric pattern that suits your dog's personality.

You Will Need

- 2 pieces of L-shaped deck-composite material, 8' long
- 1 piece of deck-composite material, 8' long and 5" wide
- 1 piece of deck-composite material, 8' long and 10" wide
- Waterproof fabric
- Finials
- Safety glasses
- Tape measure
- Pencil
- Miter saw
- Corner clamp
- Composite screws
- Jigsaw
- Sewing machine
- Thread
- Stainless steel upholstery nails
- Electric drill

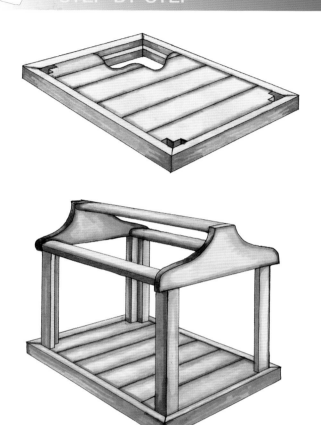

MADE IN THE SHADE
STEP BY STEP

1 This project uses a recycled, composite material from a home store. To build the base of the structure, from the L-shaped composite material cut two pieces to 36" and two pieces to 30". Make the cuts with the miter saw by cutting 45° miters into each end.

2 Use the corner clamp to assemble the base frame of the structure. The clamp holds the two pieces of material at a 45° angle (photo A).

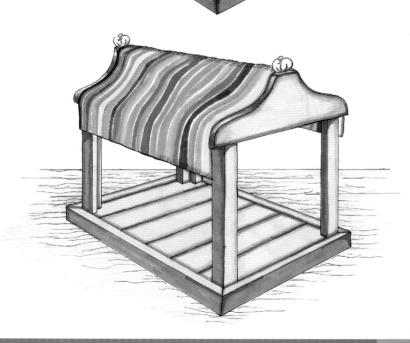

A MADE-IN-THE-SHADE STRUCTURE

DESIGN DECISIONS

With no trees or other source of shade in their yard, Gizmo and Rocky need a way to get relief from the sun because they're outside all day. Their hangout will provide a lot of shade and allow air to circulate through the structure. The house without walls will be outdoors year-round, so it's best to use durable composite deck material, which doesn't need to be weatherproofed or painted. The shade will come from a piece of outdoor upholstery fabric that's water-resistant.

MAKING A HOUSE A HOME

Building tip: The key to the structure is its composite decking, available at most home stores. The material comes in varied shapes and colors and is easy to cut.

Estimated building time: 4-6 hours

A DOG'S LIFE

Tearstains are brown discolorations around the eyes caused by bacteria on the skin that turn tears brown. In poodles, the condition is harmless. Excessive tearstains can be a symptom of other problems and should be checked by a veterinarian. In Shih Tzus, for example, tearstains may be increased by an eyelash irritating the eye, or the eyelids may be rolled inward.

A FRIENDLY BONE TO PICK

It's easy to create a first aid kit for your dog. An antiseptic solution to flush out cuts and lacerations is important. Use an antibiotic ointment to cover the wound and decrease the risk of infection. Bandages and tape to bind them should be included. Scissors, tweezers, eyedrops and a flashlight also may be useful. Make sure the kit contains emergency information with your name and phone number, your veterinarian's name and any special medical needs of the dog.

DOG TALES

■ Shih Tzus can be hard to housetrain, but they come around with consistent, patient encouragement.

■ Poodles' kneecaps sometimes pop out of joint. The problem can lead to arthritis and may need to be treated.

3 Use the special screws that accompany the composite material. The screws are threaded on the bottom with a wider thread and at the top with a finer thread to minimize "mushrooming" of the material (when the material mushrooms up around the head of the screw). Drill pilot holes first.

4 Once the frame is assembled, measure the frame's dimension, and cut the floor planks to length with the miter saw.

5 Spread the pieces of the flooring material, and on the two end pieces that cover the corners, use a piece of the L-shaped composite material to trace the points that will be notched for the upright legs (photo B).

6 With the jigsaw, cut out the notches for the uprights (photos C and D). Then install the floor, pre-drilling pilot holes and using the composite-material screws. Be sure to leave a space of $\frac{1}{8}$" to $\frac{1}{4}$" between the boards to allow for drainage.

7 Cut four pieces of the L-shaped material to 20" for the uprights. Insert the pieces into the four corners where you notched out the floorboards.

8 To make the roof's gable, trace a design on a piece of 10"-wide composite board (photo E). Once you've created the gable's layout, use the jigsaw to cut out the design. You can use the first gable as the template for the second one.

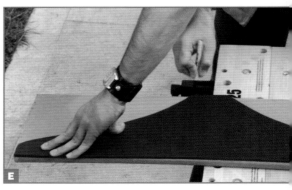

TIPS DIY Network
Home Improvement

COLOR COORDINATION
Decking screws like the ones used in the shade structure are available in different colors. When buying materials, look for screws that match the colors of the composite material or the upholstery you've chosen.

TRAINING YOUR DOG

One of the most important things you can do to ensure that you and your dog live happily together is to train it well. Training should begin from the first day the dog joins your family. For this reason, it's often a good idea to research the breed of dog you're interested in before bringing him home. Some breeds learn faster than others. By doing a little homework, you'll have a better idea of how to train your new pet, and how long to expect that training to take.

While training your dog, remember to keep an upbeat attitude and be patient, as cheerfulness and repetition are two keys to success. Whatever you do, don't punish your dog out of anger; this will make him afraid of you and could lead to aggression issues. Keep in mind that your dog wants you to like him, and as a pack animal, he wants to play by the rules you put in place. Both you and your dog will be much happier if the rules are set early and constantly reinforced. For more help with training, ask your veterinarian to direct you to local training clubs or classes.

9 The roof stringers, which will go between the front and back gables, are made from 3" x 1" composite material. Cut three pieces to 36" with the miter saw.

10 Attach stringers to the top of the uprights from front to back (photos F and G).

11 Attach the gables to the outside of the ends of the uprights in the front and back of the structure.

12 Then attach the third stringer between the top and center of the gables.

13 The structure's roof is made from a heavy-gauge, waterproof, outdoor material. The design is your choice. Starting with a piece that is 44 x 37, use a sewing machine to hem about ½" onto the edges of the material.

14 With the stainless steel upholstery nails, secure the fabric on the structure.

15 Drill a hole on either end of the center of the roof's ridge. Insert a finial into both holes for decoration (photos H and I).

ROOM WITH A VIEW

How's this for a new room with a view? Your pooch will have the best perch from which to survey the neighborhood. And if your pet happens to be an Australian cattle dog, or another breed accustomed to high places, all the better.

◀ **PROJECT SUMMARY** ▶

You'll build this treehouse in two phases. First, the deck is constructed from pressure-treated boards, then you create the house that goes on top. You'll put exterior siding and corrugated roofing on the house and paint it. A ramp will give your dog access to its lofty new home.

You Will Need

- Sand
- Pavers
- Two pieces of 2 x 6 pressure-treated lumber, 8' long
- A piece of 2 x 4 pressure-treated lumber, 8' long
- Six pieces of 1 x 6 pressure-treated lumber, 8' long
- A piece of 4 x 4 pressure-treated lumber, 8' long
- Two pieces of 2 x 3 pine, 8' long
- Three 6" hex head lag bolts
- A sheet of ½" exterior-grade siding
- A sheet of desired roofing
- Exterior paint
- Safety glasses
- Tape measure
- Chop saw
- Decking screws
- Electric drill
- Level
- Circular saw
- Jigsaw
- Paintbrush
- Caulk gun with construction adhesive

ROOM WITH A VIEW
STEP BY STEP

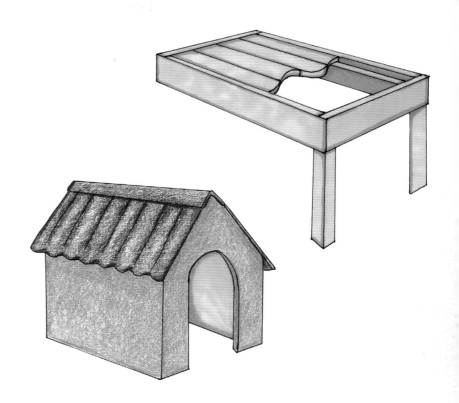

1 Cut out 2 x 6 pressure-treated lumber for the frame of the deck: 2 at 45" and 2 at 96" (photo A). Assemble with 3" galvanized deck screws.

A

UP IN THE TREES

DESIGN DECISIONS

A big backyard with lots of trees invites a treehouse. The house keeps dogs from mud and is a great addition to the property. The walls are made of exterior-grade siding, and exterior-grade paint repels the elements. A ramp, with treads to prevent slipping, provides access to the house. And in warmer months, shade from the trees keeps your dog cooler.

MAKING A HOUSE A HOME

Building tips: Increase the building's stability by connecting the frame to the tree with large lag bolts. Use galvanized bolts to avoid rusting and hurting the tree.

Estimated building time: 10–12 hours

A DOG'S LIFE

You may try several strategies to address bad behavior that's intended to get attention. Give your dog a lot of attention when he's being good. Exercise your pooch regularly to expel excess energy and to give him opportunities to do things you can praise.

A FRIENDLY BONE TO PICK

Weight loss for dogs should be slow and steady. In addition to exercise, figure on giving your dog 20 calories per pound each day. A 40-pound dog should have 800 calories a day or less if he isn't very active.

DOG TALES

▬ The Australian cattle dog is a relatively new breed. It was developed because sheepdogs of the British Isles lacked stamina for the Australian outback.

▬ The breeds involved in developing the Australian cattle dog are debated.

2 Cut pressure-treated 2 x 4 material for joists at the deck. Cut four at 45" long, then set them flush to the bottom edge of the frame, and attach with deck screws (photo B).

3 Measure and cut 1" pressure-treated decking material for the deck surface. Then attach with deck screws (photo C).

4 Level the ground where the house will be placed on the tree. Spread sand about 2" deep, and place the pavers on top of the sand (photo D). Make the paver area slightly larger than the overall dimension of the deck.

5 Cut two 4 x 4 posts to the desired height, and attach them to the underside of the deck at the front corners (photo E). Stand the deck in position, with the back edge of the deck against the tree and the two 4 x 4 posts on the pavers.

6 Drill two pilot holes through the 2 x 6 deck frame where the deck intersects the tree.

7 Drive two 6" lag bolts through the deck frame into the tree trunk. This holds the deck in place (photo F).

8 The next step is to start building the house. With 2 x 3 material, cut four pieces at 30" for the sidewalls of the frame, and cut eight pieces at 21". Four pieces are for the corner posts, and four are for stretchers at both the front and rear of the house. Use decking screws to assemble the bottom and top frames (photo G), and then attach the corner posts between the top and bottom (photo H).

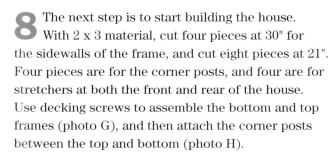

9 Measure and cut the plywood for the sides, front and back pieces at 24 x 30 for the sides. Measure the front and back of the frame to ensure a proper fit. Cut and attach (photos I, J and K).

10 Measure and cut the roof out of corrugated material. Be sure to add enough material to each dimension for a 2" overhang on each end and on the sides. Attach the roofing with screws, and be careful not to tighten the screws so much that the head penetrates the roofing (photo L). Cut the ridge vent to length and attach. Paint the roof and house as desired.

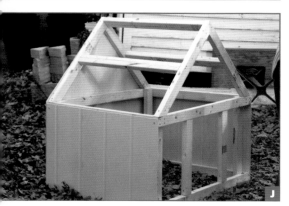

11 Measure for the ramp by beginning at the top of the deck at the front and extending to the ground. The angle of the ramp should be no more than 45°.

12 Cut the rails from 2 x 6 pressure-treated lumber. Cut five stretchers at the desired width. Assemble to complete the frame of the ramp. Measure the ramp surface, and then cut and attach ½" pressure-treated plywood.

13 Cut the strips for the tread surface. Space them evenly, and attach the strips to the top of the ramp (photo M).

REPLICA HOME

Have fun building a miniature copy of your own house, right down to the decorative trim and paint! Though it's on a smaller scale, what better way to make your dog feel at home?

◄ PROJECT SUMMARY ►

You'll start by building the plywood floor with pressure-treated 2 x 4s. Assembling the roof trusses is simple when you finish with the cut list. After you cover the roof with tarpaper and shingles, you'll attach siding and a faux brick front. A triangle cut from pine shelving and attached at the top of the doorway adds a decorative flair.

REPLICA HOME
STEP BY STEP

You Will Need

- 20 pressure-treated 2 x 4s
- 5 sheets of ¼" 4 x 8 plywood
- Roofing shingles
- Tarpaper
- Desired vinyl siding
- A 4 x 8 sheet of faux brick front
- Desired pine shelving
- Spray paint
- Safety glasses
- Tape measure
- Pencil
- Square
- Miter saw
- Pneumatic nail gun
- Chalk line
- Circular saw
- Hammer
- Shears
- Construction adhesive
- Reciprocating saw
- Jigsaw

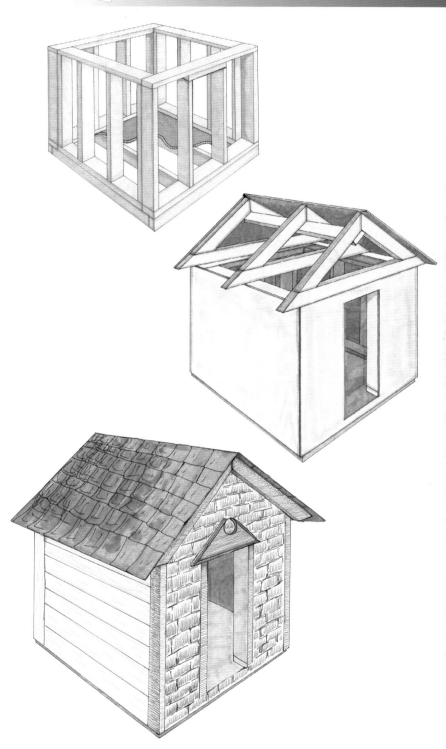

1 Cut the 2 x 4s and plywood for the frame and floor with the table saw. Cut the materials as follows:

- 2 pieces 48"
- 2 pieces 44½"
- 1 piece 48" squared
(the plywood for the floor)

MAKING A MINIATURE

DESIGN DECISIONS

Tyson is leaving an animal shelter to start his new life, so it's important that he feels at home with both his new human family and his canine roommate. A replica of the family's house reflects the concept that there's no better place than home. Building a miniature takes the same steps as constructing any house: foundation, floor, walls, roof trusses, siding and brick.

MAKING A HOUSE A HOME

Building tip: Scaling your house down to doggie-sized proportions is fun and easy. Be sure to use the helpful conversion directions supplied below before you begin.

Estimated building time: 10–12 hours

REPLICATING YOUR OWN HOME

If you want to make a smaller version of your own house for your dog, draw the original house with all the correct measurements, so you can fit it on the paper you're using. Include only the exterior measurements you will reproduce in the smaller house, and don't worry about measuring small things such as trim and molding. Use the architect's scale or your ruler, and assume that ¼" equals 1' (1:48), so a 12' long wall is 3" long on paper. If your house is too large to fit on paper at ¼" scale, use a smaller scale like ³⁄₁₆" equals 1' (1:64) or ⅛" equals 1' (1:96). It helps to draw a few different views of the house, including from the front, side and top, so you can see all the correct measurements and layout.

After you've drawn the house with full-size measurements, it's time to change the scale and proportion to fit the new occupant. The size and proportion of the new house depend on your dog's size. An exact replica of your home is not realistic if you want your pet to be able to use the front door. You need to re-size the entrance, height, length, and width of the house to suit your dog while keeping in mind the structure's original design. Using the scale 1" equals 1' (1:12) and 1½" equals 1' (1:8) or bigger, depending on the size of your house, change the measurements and proportions of the drawing to fit your dog. You may need to estimate, erase and redraw to get the right size and feel. Now you have the basic plans for your dog's new custom-scaled house.

A FRIENDLY BONE TO PICK

There are reasons to spay and neuter your pets besides reducing unwanted pregnancies. For female dogs, spaying before their second heat can reduce the risk of mammary cancer and uterine infections. Neutering males decreases the risk of prostate infections and cancer.

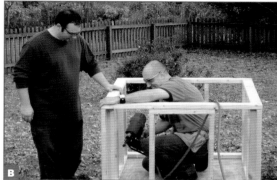

2 After the timbers are cut and connected (photo A), attach the plywood floor by screwing it down.

3 Frame the walls with 2 x 4s by making these cuts and attaching them (photo B):

- For the front and back walls, 4 at 41"
- For the side walls, 4 at 48"
- For support between the walls, 14 at 27"
- For the doorway studs, 2 at 25¼"
- For the doorway header, 1 at 20"

4 For the walls, cover all sides with plywood cut to size (photo C).

5 Here's the cut list and additional directions for the roof trusses.

- 6 at 46" with 45° angles miter-cut on each side. That will allow them to fit together at the top and with the three 54" bases.

- 3 at 52" with 45° angles cut in them. They must be 4" longer than the house frame to get a 2" overhang on both sides.

- 2 plywood triangles cut at 54" at the base. Make them with 45° cuts all the way to the top corner, so they fit over the ends of the front and back truss (photo D). Attach the trusses to the frame (photo E).

6 To cover the roof after the trusses are in place, you need two pieces of plywood. Cut one 54 x 48, and cut the other 54 x 48½ so it overlaps at the top of the structure (photo F).

7 Roll out the tarpaper, and cut it to size with the utility knife. Cover the entire roof area with tarpaper, and then nail it down with roofing nails.

8 Start adding the shingles. Remember when applying shingles to start from the bottom and work your way up so the top is always overlapping the one underneath. Make sure to stagger the seams. These measures help prevent leaking. Place the first shingles on the roof, and nail them in place with shingle nails on the top part of the shingle only. The nails will be covered by the next row of shingles. For the ridge of the roof, cover it with drop (leftover) shingles that will straddle the ridge. Then nail them in place (photo G).

9 To install the siding, attach the starter strip at the bottom of the house, and screw it in place. Attach the "J" channels on the sides of the house, so the siding can slide into them. Start at the bottom, and work your way up (photo H). Make sure not to screw each piece too tightly because weather changes can cause the wood to expand and contract, which could warp the siding. After the walls are covered, attach the corner pieces that will finish off the siding.

10 For the faux brick front, we started with a 4 x 8 sheet bought at a home-supply store. Cut the sheet to fit the front of the house. To attach the brick, apply construction adhesive (photo I), and finish with the finish nailer and some ¾" finish nails.

11 With the reciprocating saw, cut out the door between the studs on the front wall (photo J). To get started with the saw, make some holes in the corners of the door with a drill bit that is at least big enough for the saw blade to get through. That will be 17" in from either corner and up to 25¼" from the floor.

12 Now it's time to add decorative trim. With pine shelving, cut out a triangle to whatever size you choose. To add flair, mark a circle at the crest of the triangle. Cut out the circle with the jigsaw. Once the piece is done, use the trim as you wish, and attach it to the top of the doorway with the finish nailer (photo K). Then paint it as you choose.

HAPPY CAMPERS

Here's a home that appeals to the vacationing spirit in every dog. This house really suggests relaxation. Let your pooch enjoy its wanderlust right at home. You can even move the location of the camper (without the dog inside) within your yard to give your pet a change of scenery.

◢ PROJECT SUMMARY ◣

This shiny camper will certainly catch the eye of dogs and their owners alike. Using plywood laminated with sheet aluminum for the sides, more aluminum for the roof, tin for the back porch, a ball hitch and a corrugated tin awning over the entrance, you might be tempted to hang out in the camper yourself! And the floor is easy to remove for cleaning.

You Will Need

- Two ½" sheets of 4 x 8 plywood
- 2 sheets of aluminum, 4 x 8
- Two 2 x 4s, 8' long
- ½" all-thread for axle
- Wheels
- Trailer hitch
- Safety glasses
- Table saw
- Contact cement
- Paintbrushes
- Jigsaw
- Sander
- Utility knife
- Silicone adhesive
- Square
- ½" drill bit
- Caulk gun
- Aluminum screws
- Electric drill
- Hammer
- Sawhorses
- ¾" washers and nuts

HAPPY CAMPERS
STEP BY STEP

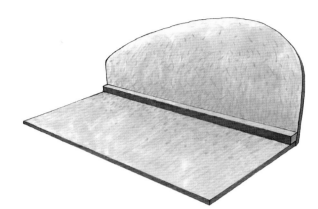

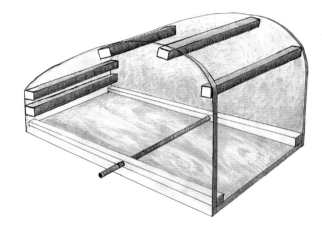

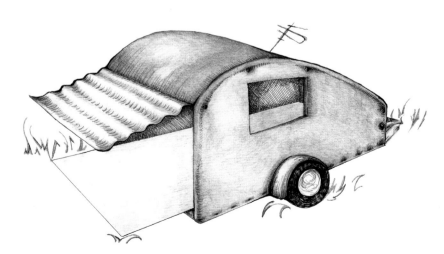

1 Cut the ½" plywood into the pieces you'll need for the floor and walls of the house. The subfloor will be a piece that is 42 x 26, and the two walls will be cut to 42 x 24. Next, rip in half a 42" piece of 2 x 4 on the table saw to create the cleats for the subfloor (photo A).

A

TRAVELIN' GUYS

DESIGN DECISIONS

The two dogs will live in the house with their family, so they need a camper for "vacations." A double-wide size will accommodate the terrier and pointer mixes. The camper, with a retro look for a vintage feel, has a removable floor for cleaning. Picture windows allow for fresh air.

MAKING A HOUSE A HOME

Estimated building time:
10–12 hours

A FRIENDLY BONE TO PICK

One of the most important factors in choosing dog food is to give your dog the right diet for his age and size. Make sure you read the labels carefully. One of the top three ingredients should be a meat or meat byproduct. Meat helps keep coats healthy and shiny.

A DOG'S LIFE

To train a dog, start with basic commands to sit, stay and walk on a leash. Do it every day with consistency and repetition for 10 to 15 minutes.

DOG TALES

The tallest breed is the Irish wolfhound, which is 34" at the shoulders. The shortest breed is the Chihuahua, which is 6" to 9" at the shoulders.

2 Attach the cleats to the long sides of the subfloor with 2" wood screws (photo B). An additional piece of plywood must be cut for the removable floor, which should be 24 x 54, so it hangs out the front of the house and creates a porch for the pooches.

3 To attach the aluminum sheeting to the walls, apply contact cement on the aluminum and plywood (photo C). Evenly coat both pieces, and let them sit for about five minutes until the color of the cement changes from clear to a milky white; the cement will be tacky to the touch. Flip the aluminum onto the wood, and push it firmly into place. The bond is instant and permanent. Make sure to leave a ¾" overlap in the aluminum at the base of the wall. The aluminum's dimensions should be 24¾ x 42. The floor of the house is sheeted with the aluminum the same way.

4 Shape a template for the walls from hardboard or cardboard using any shape you choose. Place the template on the glued aluminum and wood wall, and mark the shape with a scribe or utility knife (photo D).

5 Use the jigsaw with a metal-cutting blade to cut out the shape of the wall. After the wall is cut, use the belt-sander to smooth out all the edges (photo E).

6 For the window of the camper, you may use any size or shape. We used an 8 x 10 aluminum, store-bought picture frame. Scribe the shape into the wall at your desired location (photo F).

7 Use a drill with the ¾" paddle bit to make holes in two corners, so the jigsaw can cut out the window opening (photo G). After cutting the hole, set the frame in place, and seal it there with silver silicone adhesive.

8 To attach the walls, first mark a hole pattern 1¾" from the bottom of the wall along its length. This will allow it to clear the subfloor and screw into the center of the ripped 2 x 4. Pre-drill through the marks with a ⅛" drill bit to make holes to attach the walls with 2" wood screws to the subfloor cleats. Repeat for both sidewalls.

9 Cut 2 x 4 crossbars to 24" long to fit between the walls as supports. Line them up at the top of the walls with the pre-drilled holes and attach (photo H).

10 Next, go back to the aluminum overhang at the bottom of the walls. With the hammer, gently hit the overhanging aluminum to lightly bend it beneath the floor to add security and seal the bottom.

11 The roof is made from a piece of the aluminum sheeting that is about 1½" wider than the house. To attach the roof, flip the structure upside down, and attach one end of the aluminum roof to the subfloor.

12 Flip the entire structure over again (photo I), and attach the aluminum to the top of the house with aluminum screws (photo J). Make sure there are no gaps between the walls and the roof. Next, hammer the overhang down over the wall as you did to the bottom of the walls.

13 To add the wheels, measure from one end of the trailer to the center of the trailer, and go up ¾" from the bottom to clear the subfloor. Drill a ¾" hole on both sides of the trailer with a paddle bit.

14 Through the hole on both sides, insert the bar of all-thread to be used as the axle (photo K), and attach the wheels to the axle with washers and nuts (photo L).

15 Using drop sheets of aluminum, cut out pieces to attach over the wheels as fenders for the real camper look. The fenders, attached with the aluminum screws, can be shaped as desired.

16 The trailer hitch assembly is built with a ripped 2 x 4 structure and a store-bought hitch. Rip a 2 x 4 in half, and create a "Y" from the pieces. The two pieces that come in from the sides need miter cuts at 45° on the ends that connect to the center piece (photo M). Attach the assembly to the trailer with 2" wood screws.

17 Now, add the corrugated tin awning over the entrance to the house (photo N). Cut a piece of tin with tin snips to 24 x 24. Attach it to the house with aluminum screws, and support it with metal dowels that attach to the floor and awning. **Note: Only pull the trailer at a slow crawl and never with a pet inside!**

RUFFING IT

For a dog who loves to travel, this is the place! Whether hobo or first-class traveler, the tent is a great place to come home to. It's easy to build and clean, and the materials aren't expensive. This tent is also small enough to move around for a change in scenery.

◀ **PROJECT SUMMARY** ▶

Building this project begins with the base, which is made of made of pressure-treated 2 x 4s. The frame is made of copper tubing. The outer surface will be three pieces of oiled canvas, one each for the front and back walls and one for the top and sides. Copper rivets will hold the structure together. The awning can be tied up for nice weather or put down to help protect your dog from the elements.

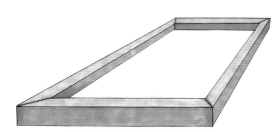

RUFFING IT
STEP BY STEP

You Will Need

- 2 pressure-treated 2 x 4s, 8' long
- 1 piece of 24 x 36 pine shelving
- 3 pieces of ¾" copper tubing, 8' long
- ¾" copper fittings: 12 T-fittings, six 120° fittings, three 90° fittings
- Heavy-duty canvas
- Safety glasses
- Pencil
- Measuring tape
- Miter saw
- 3" screws
- Electric drill
- Square
- ⅞" paddle bit
- Polyurethane
- Paintbrush
- Tubing cutter
- Soldering paste
- Soldering torch
- Sandpaper
- Clamps
- Rivets
- Rivet gun
- Utility knife
- Straightedge

1 With the miter saw, cut 2 x 4s on edge for a 24 x 36 floor with mitered 45° corners. Using the 3" wood screws, attach at the mitered corners.

SIMBA VS. NATURE

DESIGN DECISIONS

As a terrier mix with a history of behavioral problems, Simba needs a house that reflects his active lifestyle. A tent is easy to build and not expensive. Even while accommodating Simba's height of 17" at the shoulders, the tent is small enough to pick up to clean or move.

MAKING A HOUSE A HOME

Building tip: If you plan to leave the tent in one place outdoors for awhile, consider building a platform with pavers. This will keep the area cleaner and the tent base lasting longer.

Estimated building time: 4-6 hours

A FRIENDLY BONE TO PICK

Fleas and ticks cause the most skin problems for dogs. A product that kills eggs and adult fleas is most effective. Monthly topical drops help, too. Sprays and foggers are good for the house, but if you have cats be sure the product is OK to use. Use forceps to remove ticks, and dispose of them in a jar of alcohol or bleach.

A DOG'S LIFE

Terriers can be very active and prone to barking, digging, and running away. It helps to adjust the dogs to using a collar and leash. To address dominance issues, it may be useful to roll the dog over on his back, and stare at him until he looks away.

DOG TALES

Behavioral problems often start with boredom. Neutering and spaying and giving the dog a lot of attention can address the problems.

If you establish clearly what is and isn't acceptable, the dog will learn what is expected and will want to please.

2 Attach the pine floor to the 2 x 4 frame with the 3" wood screws (photo A).

3 Next, drill the holes for the copper tubing to be set into the pine floor. With the ⅞" spade drill bit, drill holes on all four corners ¾" from the edges at the corners (photo B). Drill holes in the center of the flooring on both sides.

4 Use polyurethane to seal the base of the tent. If you live in an area that gets a lot of rain, a few coats of polyurethane are recommended.

5 Cut the copper tubing with a pipe cutter to the following lengths (photo C).

Cut list:
- 6 pieces 18¾" (uprights)
- 2 pieces 22" (front and back crossbars)
- 4 pieces 23" (sides)
- 12 pieces 1½" (couplers for fittings)

6 Clean the ends of the tubing and the inside surface of all fittings with the sandpaper or scrubber pads. Assemble the front and back walls of the frame.

TIPS | DIY Network Home Improvement

WARPING

Make sure to coat with polyurethane both sides of the pine boards for the tent's floor. If only one side is coated, the boards will "cup." This warping is caused by moisture on the damp, uncoated side, and eventually could lead to the boards being cracked and in need of replacement.

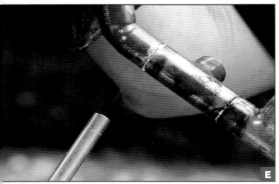

7 Cut the canvas for the front and back walls of the house using the assembled frame as the template (photo D). Use the straightedge to mark the canvas, and leave 4" of excess around all the sides. The canvas should be doubled over before you cut so that you cut out both ends at the same time. Cut out the canvas with the sharp razor knife.

8 Flux and sweat all the fittings and pieces for the frame. Apply a light coat of soldering paste or flux to the cleaned end of the copper. Use a flux brush or an old toothbrush to spread the flux. Place the copper fitting on the pipe after thoroughly cleaning and coating with flux. With the soldering torch, place flame all around the fitting to bring up to soldering heat. Then concentrate the flame at the center of the fitting (photo E). After properly heated, apply the solder to the heated area. The solder will flow into the seams of the connection. Keep melting the solder until it appears completely around the fitting. Do this for all fittings of the frame.

9 For the back wall and middle (interior) wall, place the canvas on a wall frame, making sure that the wall of canvas is on the outside of the frame. Hold it in place with a clamp at the crest of the roofline.

10 Fold the edge of the canvas over about 1", and then fold the excess over the tubing to meet the wall of canvas. With the drill, make ⅛" holes in the canvas every 6" along the wall (photo F); these will be rivet points.

11 Place the rivet into the rivet gun, and rivet the canvas (photo G). Make sure the canvas is pulled tightly along the wall because the canvas will stretch eventually.

12 For the roof and side walls of the tent, cut a piece of canvas to 56 x 90, and drape it over the frame, centering the canvas on the roofline.

13 Roll up the excess material at the base of one side of the structure. Attach the canvas to the base, or floor, of the house with 1" wood screws at the rear corner and at the center pole on one side. Then pull the canvas tightly over the house, and repeat the process on the other side (photo H).

14 To create the awning effect, use the razor knife to cut the canvas along the center pole from the bottom of the material to the bottom of the roofline. The awning can be tied up for nice weather or let down to protect your dog from the weather.

15 The front roof section is attached to the frame the same way the walls were attached, by folding the canvas over and riveting it about every 6".

16 Cut a slit in the center of the interior wall to create the door (photo I), and you're ready to make camp.

3

Beyond Houses

Dogs' needs, just like those of people, extend beyond housing. This chapter offers a variety of projects to improve the comfort of your canine friend. On the practical side, you'll find a decorative gate, a water trough, a food storage cabinet, a crate, and a dog run. For looks and comfort, you'll also find a lounge bed and a step stool seat. Although each project can be made exactly as directed, feel free to let your creativity and your dog's personality alter the projects. Add steps to the stool if your dog likes to sit under a high window, or change the shape of the water trough if your pooch is a smaller breed and a little daintier when drinking.

GATED COMMUNITY

This is a great idea for homes on a busy street. You can keep your dog from playing in traffic and have a place where your family can hang out with your pet. By enclosing the porch with gates and adding a lounge for your pooch, your dog will have a perfect – and safe – way to watch people, cars, and dogs passing by.

◀ PROJECT SUMMARY ▶

These classy gates feature a forged, decorative pin that slides through the guide into the porch. You'll build two frames for the gate and a frame for the lounge, all out of tubular metal. The pieces are cut and welded together. A cushion on the lounge gives your dog a place to relax in style and comfort.

You Will Need

- 4 pieces of 1" tubular metal, each 8' long
- 60 pieces of ¼" roundstock at 14" long
- Weatherproof spray paint
- Desired hinges and door latch
- Safety glasses
- Tape measure
- Pencil
- Chop saw
- Metal-cutting chopsaw
- Clamps
- Flux-core welder
- Grinder
- Ear protection
- Vice
- Electric drill
- Door hinges
- Door lock mechanism
- Welding visor

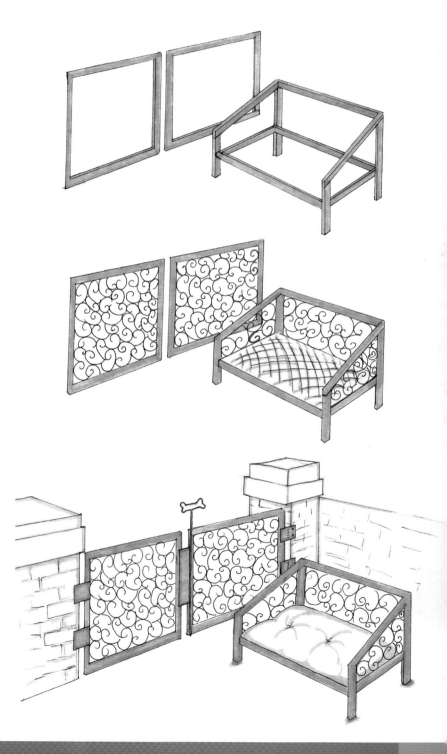

1 Cut all the metal pieces required. You'll need four pieces of 1" square steel tubing cut to 24" long and then miter-cut at 45° on both ends. Cut four pieces at 36" long with miter cuts of 45° at the ends. Use a metal cutting chop saw with an abrasive blade designed to cut metal. The combined width of the gates will be 72".

2 Arrange the cut pieces in the shape of the gate's frame. To create the frame, use two of the 36" pieces, one each at the top and bottom, and then 24" pieces for both sides. With the miter cuts, the pieces fit together.

LOUNGING AROUND

DESIGN DECISIONS

The gate and lounger are particularly good for dogs who like to roam and people-watch. The metal gate keeps your dog at home, and the matching lounger is a place for your pooch to perch so everyone can relax together. The gate's two frames and the lounger's frame are made from tubular metal. For a decorative touch, a forged metal pin slides through the gate's guide and into the porch. A cushion on the lounger adds comfort and style.

MAKING A HOUSE A HOME

Building tips: Different sizes of scrolls enhance the gate's appearance. To create smaller scrolls, pull the metal more tightly around the jig. For larger scrolls, don't pull the metal as tightly.

Estimated building time: 8-10 hours

A DOG'S LIFE

Being spayed before the age of 2 decreases a dog's risk of mammary cancer. If your dog is older, you should check every month or two for lumps along the glands on her chest. If you find lumps, a veterinarian can do a biopsy by removing tissue to check for disease.

A FRIENDLY BONE TO PICK

Be sure to keep poisons in the garage away from your dog's reach. Drinking antifreeze can cause kidney damage or death. Some motor oils and auto cleansers induce vomiting. Rat poison can cause serious bleeding, and other pest baits can bring on seizures.

DOG TALES

One female dog and her offspring can produce 67,000 dogs in six years. Spaying and neutering animals can help prevent that.

3 Weld all four corners of one of the gates with a flux-core welder, which you can rent from a building-equipment business. To make the welds, clamp the grounding clamp to the piece of metal you're welding. Pull the trigger on the welder, which creates an arc and completes the circuit, melting the wire that welds the metal pieces together. Weld the four corners (photo A), and repeat for the second gate.

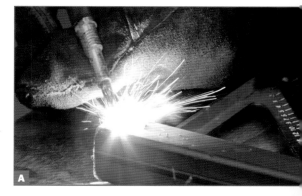

4 Use an angle grinder with an abrasive grinding wheel to smooth any rough spots from the welds (photo B). Hold the grinder so the wheel is at a slight angle to the metal. The wheel's speed and the grinder's weight will do most of the work, so hold the grinder tightly.

5 The easiest way to bend the ¼" roundstock for the decorative scrolls is to create a jig. To make the jig, drill a ¼" hole about 1" down from one end of a 6" piece of 1½" steel tubing. Clamp the tubing into a vice as tightly as you can, so it won't move around when bending. Cut about 60 pieces of ¼" roundstock into 14" lengths. Put one end of the ¼" roundstock into the ¼" hole on the jig, and bend the stock into the desired scroll shape (photo C). Bending the stock tightly around the jig creates a smaller scroll; bending it loosely makes a larger scroll. Repeat as needed.

6 To weld the scrolls in place and fill the frame, center the scrolls on the width of the 1" frame with a piece of ½" plywood set within the frame. Arrange the scrolls within the frame, and make sure they touch other scrolls or the frame at three points. When the frame is filled, weld the scrolls into place with the flux-core welder (photo D).

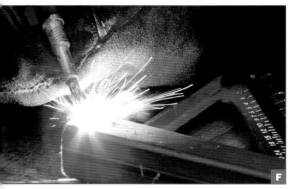

7 Finish the gates by spray-painting them with outdoor-grade paint. At least two coats are recommended to protect the gates from the weather.

8 To install the gates, use a grinder, and remove the paint on one side of the gate where it will attach to the wall (photo E). Then attach the hinges. If you use metal hinges, weld them to the gate. Paint the hinges to match the gate.

9 Weld the 3" sleeves for the locking pin on the inside end of one of the gates. The sleeve is the tube that the locking pin will slide into and then into the ground to lock the gate. If you use ½" steel roundstock for the pin, the sleeve should be larger than ½" in diameter. Attach the locking mechanism you've chosen.

10 Drill pilot holes onto the brick posts (photo F), and mount the gates with the hinges that were welded to the gates (photo G). Drill a hole into the concrete for the locking pin.

11 For the lounger, cut all of the pieces you need (photo H). Two legs will be cut at 9" long and two legs at 12". Cut two stretchers at 12" and two stretchers at 14". Cut three rails at 24" long.

12 After all the pieces are cut, assemble and weld the sidewalls. You'll need a 9" leg in front and a 12" leg in back. You will also need a 12" stretcher 4" from the bottom of the legs to support the lounger, and a 14" stretcher at the top to connect the 9" leg and 12" leg.

13 Now use the three 24" rails to connect the sidewalls (photo I). One rail will go between the tops of the 12" back legs, and another rail will go between the back legs 4" from the bottom. The third rail goes between the front legs 4" from the bottom.

14 Use 1"-wide steel flat stock running from the front to the back of the lounger's support. Weld the flat stock into place, and leave about 1" between them.

15 Paint the lounger with at least two coats of an outdoor-grade spray paint. Place an outdoor dog bed or pillow on the lounger supports.

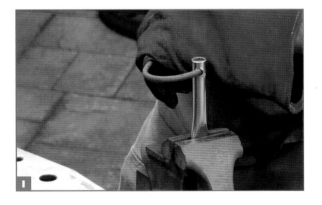

BARKLOUNGER

This attractive window seat makes a nice addition to a room in your house. It's created for dogs who stay inside a lot and like to look out the window. Consider the structure a small throne with a cushion, and let your dog daydream of royalty.

◀ **PROJECT SUMMARY** ▶

Classy and compact, this lounge is made of Baltic birch plywood. You'll cut out the side panels, steps and toe-kick, and then attach the parts. Once it's assembled, you'll add trim and then sand and stain the whole piece. After that, you'll have the fun of decorating it with appliqués as you wish.

BARKLOUNGER
STEP BY STEP

You Will Need

- 1 sheet of 4 x 4 Baltic birch plywood
- Self-adhesive veneer
- Desired base molding
- Desired decorative trim
- Cushion
- Safety glasses
- Pencil
- Tape measure
- Table saw
- Clamps
- Jigsaw
- Chop saw
- Wood glue
- Pneumatic nail gun
- Spring punch
- Wood filler
- Wood stain
- Paintbrush
- Veneer trim tool
- Utility knife
- Random orbit sander
- Gilding paste

1 Cut out the sides for the lounger from a piece of ½" Baltic birch. Cut two pieces 10 x 21.

2 Mark the following riser/side panel dimensions on one piece of the plywood: from the bottom left corner go up 5", run 10½" to the right, and then go up 5". Clamp both 10 x 21 pieces together, and cut them out with a jigsaw following the riser layout you created.

LOUNGING AROUND

DESIGN DECISIONS

Dogs who stay inside all day may not need a doghouse. But if they like to watch the world outside the window and can't reach the window, they'll love this piece of furniture. The modified window seat with a step has a cushion, too, so your dog can hang out in comfort.

MAKING A HOUSE A HOME

Building tips: Always make a cut list first because it helps you stay organized.

Estimated building time: 6–8 hours

A DOG'S LIFE

Male dogs, especially non-neutered ones, may mark their territory indoors by leaving a urine scent. If you have multiple dogs and aren't sure which one is marking, use a diaper-like belly band to catch the culprit.

A FRIENDLY BONE TO PICK

Problems with the trachea, the airway to the lungs, are common with Yorkshire terriers. A tracheal collapse causes a severe cough and trouble with exercise. Your veterinarian can treat the condition, but make sure your dog stays slim because an overweight dog may have trouble breathing.

DOG TALES

Breeding practices to keep Yorkshire terriers tiny have created health issues. Smaller Yorkies may be prone to liver problems and other illnesses. Breeders need to be aware of the problems and educate others.

3 Cut a piece of ½" Baltic birch plywood to the following dimensions (photo A): 2 at 30 x 10½, another at 5 x 30 and one at 1¾ x 30. The pieces will be the treads and kick plate for the step lounge.

4 From scrap wood, create four cleats 10" long to assemble the lounge.

5 Glue and nail the cleats ¾" down from the 10½" runs inside both side-panel pieces (photo B).

6 Place glue on top of the cleats, and lay the 30 x 10½ treads between the side assemblies and on top of the cleats (photos C and D). Use the nail gun to fasten with pin nails.

7 Cut two more cleats 3½" long, and cut two 1¾" long. Attach the 3½" cleats with glue and nails to the inner walls of the side risers ¾" back from the front step. Then attach the 5 x 30 kick plate piece to these cleats. The two shorter cleats will be used below the top step of the lounge. Set the cleats back ¾" from the front of the top step and attach. Attach the top 1¾" kick plate to the cleats with glue and nails.

8 After the step is assembled, use wood putty to fill holes left by nails during assembly (photo E). Apply the putty with your finger, and make sure to fill each hole and smooth away the excess. Once the putty is dry, use a fine-grit sandpaper for a smooth finish.

9 Cover the edges of the plywood with self-adhesive veneer (photo F). Start by applying the veneer evenly from back to front on the exposed plywood edges, along the top and in front. Use a utility knife to trim off the excess pieces for a tight fit. After the veneer is applied, use a veneer-cutting tool along the sides (photo G), and clean up any overhang.

10 Use a decorative wood trim along the bottom of the base. Make 45° miter cuts at each end, so the trim pieces fit well together. Measure and cut pieces accordingly. Then apply a 21" piece of 1" trim aligned with the front of the top step to cover the exposed edge of the plywood. Attach it all using glue and pin nails.

11 Finish and seal the step lounge with your choice of wood stain. After it dries, decorate and attach finish appliqués as desired.

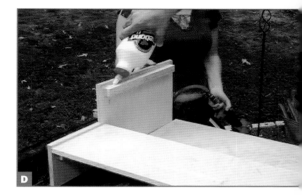
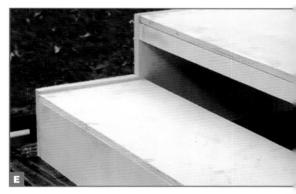
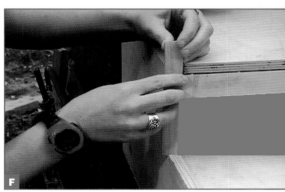
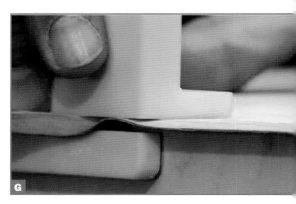

COMFY CRATE

Dog crates can be rather unattractive. They're usually made of plastic or metal fencing and used just for function. But this crate will resemble a piece of furniture. It will look cool but also be functional. The frame is made of metal with some expanded metal for the open areas to provide good ventilation. A punch-tin panel made of copper adds a decorative touch.

◀ PROJECT SUMMARY ▶

A crate is suitable for dogs that are accustomed to being transported, such as a greyhound that has retired from its racing career. But housetraining can be easier with a crate, too, because dogs don't like to soil their own space. Make sure your dog gets exercise if it's in a crate all day.

You Will Need

- Pre-cut 1½" angle iron (see step 1 for sizes)
- Pre-cut expanded metal (see step 6 for sizes)
- 27 x 24 piece of copper sheet
- 1 sheet of 24 x 36 pine shelving
- 1 4 x 8 sheet of ½" plywood
- Safety glasses
- Portable welder
- Square
- Tape measure
- Pencil
- Table saw
- Metal punch
- Wood stain
- Paintbrushes
- Miter saw
- Shop towels
- ¼" screws
- Electric drill
- Door hinges
- Door lock mechanism

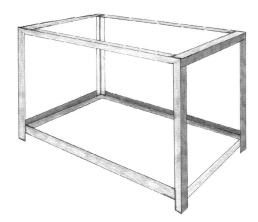

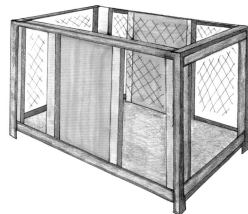

1 Cut the 1½" angle iron to the needed sizes. This can be done by your local supplier or fabricator with this cut list.

- 2 pieces 102" long
- 4 pieces 42" long
- 4 pieces 24" wide

CRAZY ABOUT HER CRATE

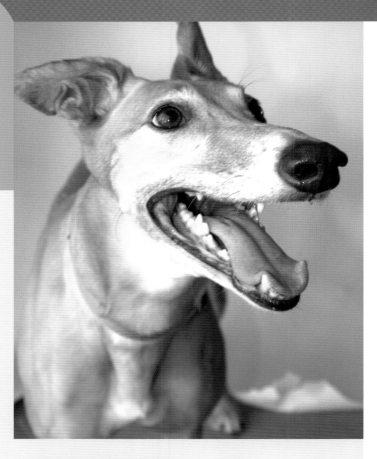

DESIGN DECISIONS

As a retired racing dog, Lily, a greyhound, is accustomed to being transported in crates. A crate is functional and can blend with the furniture in a home. A punched-tin panel on each side of the crate makes the doghouse more decorative.

MAKING A HOUSE A HOME

Building tip: You can make the process easier by ordering the metal cut to size from a supplier.

Estimated building time: 8–10 hours

A DOG'S LIFE

Exercise keeps your dog's heart fit, tones his muscles and maintains joints rich in nutrients. You can exercise your pet by walking him or throwing him a ball. But before vigorous exercise, help your dog warm up by walking or stretching. Dogs that stay in a crate all day may need more warming up.

A FRIENDLY BONE TO PICK

Crates can be helpful because they create a safe place for a dog inside your home. The structures can make it easier to housebreak your pet because a dog doesn't want to mess up its own territory. Remember to give your dog opportunities to stretch outside the crate.

DOG TALES

■ Greyhounds, bred for racing, have more red blood cells than other dogs, and their oxygen-rich blood makes them good blood donors.

■ The docile breed gets along well with other dogs. Greyhounds don't bark much and generally are well-mannered pets.

2 Cut 90° notches 30" from each end of the 102" piece of angle iron. Then bend to a 90° angle, and tack-weld at each notch (photo A). Repeat for the other side.

3 Weld the stretchers (24" long) to the top corners to connect the sides, and also weld them 3" from the bottom of the legs. Then weld 42" long rails between the legs of each wall to support the floor (photo B).

4 Shear the copper to 27 x 24, and punch your pattern of choice (photos C and D).

5 Cut the pine boards, eight pieces 3 x 27.

6 Shear the expanded metal; this can be done by your local supplier or fabricator with this cut list.

- 2 pieces 41½ x 26½ (for the sides)
- 1 piece 23½ x 41½ (for the top)
- 2 pieces 23½ x 26½ (for the back and front)

TIPS | DIY Network Home Improvement

WELDING
To make a stronger weld, bevel the edges of the pieces that will touch when welded. Beveling these edges creates a small channel between the pieces, allowing a space for welding material to flow and, due to the increased surface area, make a stronger bond. This technique also works great once you begin grinding and smoothing the weld—the joint won't weaken since the bonded material is inside the groove.

A

B

C

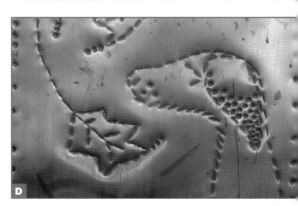

D

WELDING SAFETY

Most homeowners and casual hobbyists know what welding is even if they don't know the specifics. Most simply, it is a fabrication process used to join two pieces of a material such as metal. Often, a filler material is heated by the welder along with the pieces to be joined. This material helps to form a strong joint once it cools.

Because of the presence of an open flame, welding can be a dangerous activity if safety guides are not followed. Precautions can easily be taken to lower the risk of burns, electric shock, inhaling noxious fumes, and exposure to ultraviolet light. Wear leather gloves and long sleeves to help prevent burns. To avoid a condition called "arc eye," be sure to wear a face plate designed for welding. This will limit the amount of UV radiation reaching your eyes. It also helps to weld in an area with plenty of ventilation, as welders are often exposed to dangerous gases that are released during the heating process. And finally, be aware of your surroundings. Be sure to keep all flammable and combustible materials safely away from your welding work site.

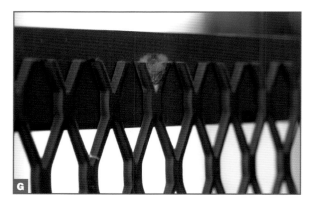

7 Stain the wood, and then attach the copper to the wood rails with ¼" screws (photo E). Next, attach the expanded metal from the back to complete the wall panels.

8 Insert the wall panels inside the completed frame, and tack-weld in place. Then do the same for the top and back (photos F and G).

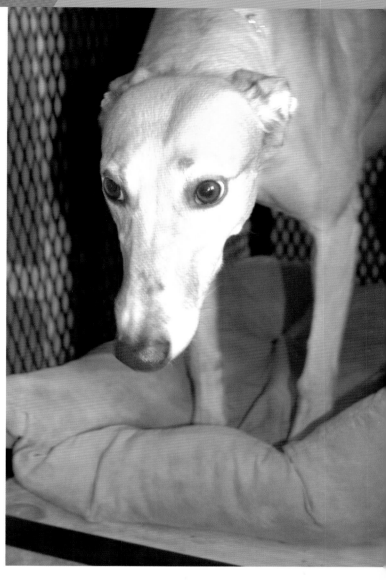

9 With a 1½ x ⅛ flat bar, weld the frame for the door at 24 x 27. Weld the expanded metal to the door frame, and weld the hinges to the door. Clamp the door to the crate, and then weld the hinges to the crate. Next, weld the latch components into place (photo H).

10 Cut the ½" plywood to 23½ x 41½ to make the floor. Insert the floor into the bottom of the crate. Add a comfortable mat or pillow that matches the room's decor, and your dog's stylish new crate is ready to use.

TIPS DIY Network Home Improvement

CARPET SAVER
Place a leftover piece of plywood or other material under the legs of your crate. This will protect your carpet or flooring from damage.

CANINE CORRAL

A dog run is great if your yard isn't fenced, providing an area for your dog to play without the need for a leash. A run is also a safe place for your pet to exercise, which helps it maintain a healthy weight.

◢ PROJECT SUMMARY ◣

Dog runs usually aren't too exciting or attractive, but yours will look great with a base of landscaping timbers and landscape fabric. A shade structure added at the end will help keep your dog cooler in warm weather. And antibacterial tiling placed over two inches of gravel will make the run cleaner.

CANINE CORRAL
STEP BY STEP

You Will Need

- 8 landscape timbers, 8' long
- Landscaping fabric, 10 x 20
- Various 2 x 2 stakes
- 8 pressure-treated 1 x 6 boards, 10' long
- 4 pressure-treated 2 x 4s, 6' long
- 4 pressure-treated 4 x 4s, 6' long
- Fencing material
- Gravel
- Door hinges
- Gate latch
- Heavy-duty corrugated vinyl
- Antibacterial mat
- Safety glasses
- Pencil
- Measuring tape
- Miter saw
- Sledgehammer
- 3" decking screws
- Staple gun
- Staples
- Wheelbarrow
- Jigsaw
- Door hinges
- Door lock mechanism

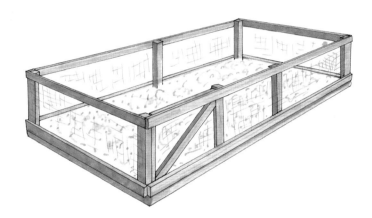

1 Cut the pieces of landscape timbers to these lengths:

- Two 4' pieces
- Six 8' pieces
- Eighteen 2 x 2 stakes to anchor the frame

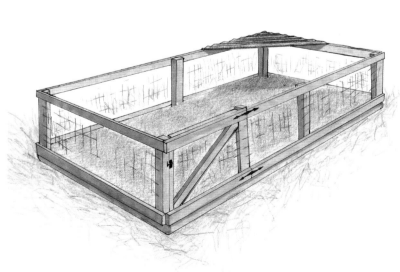

FREE TO ROAM

DESIGN DECISIONS

For dogs with a big yard but no fence, a dog run provides a way to exercise. The structure is a fenced area with enough space for dogs to run. Dog-run dimensions vary by breed and size of the dog and how much time he will spend in the run. Gravel, about 2" deep, creates a flat surface on which to place the flooring, which consists of antibacterial tiling. The tiles are easy to clean, and they wear well. The gravel and plastic flooring drain moisture from the run.

MAKING A HOUSE A HOME

Building tip: Use heavy-duty, corrugated vinyl for the shade structure. With a circular saw, cut the vinyl to size, and leave a 1½" overhang, so water will drain away from the enclosure.

Estimated building time: 12–14 hours

A DOG'S LIFE

Jack Russell terriers are energetic and love to chase, bark, chew, and dig. For those reasons, they aren't the best "starter" dogs. Staffordshire terriers are good with people but can be aggressive with other dogs and smaller pets, including cats. Staffordshire terriers are used in police work and as watchdogs.

A FRIENDLY BONE TO PICK

If you're looking for a new dog, shelters and rescue societies are great places to find a pup. There are many great pets awaiting adoption in shelters across the nation. If you're having trouble finding a specific breed in shelters, try looking on the Internet where there are many breed-specific rescue societies. These websites often include pictures and personality profiles.

DOG TALES

■ Dog runs are created as public spaces in some urban areas, and provide a place for people and dogs to enjoy the outdoors.

■ The American Kennel Club first registered American Staffordshire terriers in 1936.

2 Use the landscape fabric to create the 10 x 20 footprint of the dog run on the ground. With the landscape timbers, create the base frame along the outer edges of the fabric (photo A). Use two of the 8' pieces with a 4' piece to make up one of the 20' walls.

3 With the sledgehammer, hammer in stakes along the outside of the frame to help secure it.

4 To make the 20' wall, use two 10' 2 x 6 pieces lying end to end to make both the top and bottom runs of the wall. With the top and bottom runs lying on the ground, unroll the plastic-coated wire fencing along the 2 x 6 pieces—flush at the top and 1½" from the bottom (photo B). Attach the fence to the frame about every 8" with the staple gun.

5 Join the two 10' boards with a 4 x 4 post, using 3" deck screws.

6 Attach a 2 x 4 that is inset 3½" from both ends of the 20' wall (photo C). This will be the point where the side and back walls meet.

7 Assemble the 10' walls using the same methods as for the 20' wall, but this time use one 10' 2 x 6 for the top and bottom.

8 Attach 4 x 4 posts flush to the ends of both 10' walls (photo D).

TIPS | DIY Network Home Improvement

4 x 4 FENCE POSTS
To get extra stability and permanence from your dog run, set the treated 4 x 4 corner posts into the ground. A general rule of thumb is to bury one-third of the post's overall height, so include this estimate in your measurements. Use gravel or cement around the post for extra staying power. Tamp soil firmly around the posts to finish.

9 Set the back wall and two side walls into place. The back wall's inset 2 x 4 pieces should meet up to the end walls' flush-mounted 4 x 4 pieces. Attach on the inside at the top and bottom with 3" deck screws. Using the same screws, attach the bottom of the walls to the landscape-timber frame on the ground.

10 Fill the entire area inside the fence with 2" of gravel that is raked level.

11 Set the back wall and two side walls into place. The back wall's inset 2 x 4 pieces should meet up to the end walls' flush-mounted 4 x 4 pieces. Attach on the inside at the top and bottom with 3" deck screws. Using the same screws, attach the bottom of the walls to the landscape-timber frame on the ground.

12 Fill the entire area inside the fence with 2" of gravel that is raked level.

13 Frame the gate with 2 x 4 pressure-treated wood. Use a 45° miter cut (photo E) to make two 4' pieces for the uprights and two 32" pieces for the top and bottom. Once the frame is assembled with the deck screws, add a diagonal piece of wood from the bottom right to the top left inside the frame (photo F).

14 Attach the fencing material to the outside of the frame with the staple gun. Then add two 35¾" pieces of 1 x 6 material at the top and bottom of the outside of the gate to match the rest of the fence (photo G). The extra 3¾" of overhang on the top and bottom 1 x 6 will act as a stop for the gate.

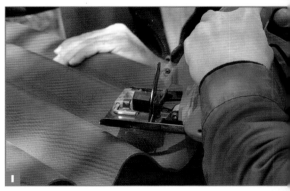

15 Attach the hinges and latch using the hardware and instructions provided with them, and then attach the gate to the 17' section of fence.

16 The shade roof is made from a sheet of heavy-duty, corrugated vinyl, which is available at home-improvement stores. Place the sheet vinyl over the top of one of the corners of the dog run (photo H). Use 1½" screws to hold it in place. Be sure to drive the screws into the valleys of the corrugated material.

17 With the circular saw, cut the excess roofing material that hangs over the outside of the corner it shades (photo I).

18 The last element is the antibacterial mat (photo J). Follow the manufacturer's instructions to put this together, and your dog run is ready.

WATER TROUGH

This structure may resemble a miniature hot tub, but it's actually a watering hole. The concrete trough offers plenty of room for hefty bulldogs— or any breed—to belly up to the bar together. You can be sure that your multiple dogs will have equal opportunity to quench their thirst, without having to fight for elbow room.

◀ **PROJECT SUMMARY** ▶

You'll start by making the exterior mold from particle board. Then you'll seal the mold's inside seams, and shape an interior mold from foam. PVC sheeting will cover the foam mold, into which you'll pour concrete. After the concrete "cures" for 10 to 14 days, you'll have a solid trough. A drainpipe and automatic watering system will ensure fresh and plentiful water for your dogs.

You Will Need

- Automatic watering system
- A 4 x 8 sheet of melamine-covered particleboard
- A 4 x 8 sheet of ¼" PVC
- Wood screws
- Polystyrene foam blank, at least 12 x 36
- Stainless steel decorations, if desired
- Silicone sealant
- Dishwashing liquid
- 2 parts sand
- 3 parts gravel
- 1 part cement
- Water
- Concrete dye in desired color
- ½" copper tubing, 8" to 10" long
- ½" rubber stopper
- Safety glasses
- Tape measure
- Electric drill
- Caulk gun
- Four 5-gallon buckets
- Concrete vibrator
- ⁹⁄₁₆" drill bit
- Cement mixer

WATER TROUGH STEP BY STEP

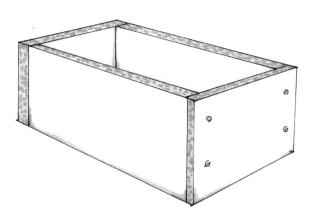

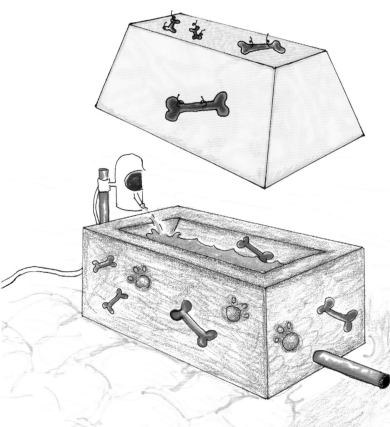

1 Build the exterior mold for the trough. Use ½" thick melamine-covered particleboard and a circular saw to make the cuts (photo A). Cut one at 13½ x 36, cut two at 10 x 36, and cut two more at 13½ x 10½.

A

DOGGIE OASIS

DESIGN DECISIONS

With five English bulldogs, making sure they all get enough water can be a challenge. A trough is a great solution, especially for a breed that can get overheated easily. An automatic watering system, which senses a dog's presence, ensures that your pooches will have plenty of the wet stuff. A drain on one end of the trough makes it easy to replace the water. It's important to clean the trough regularly, and a couple of times a week in summer, so the water will be fresh.

MAKING A HOUSE A HOME

Estimated building time:
6–8 hours for labor. The concrete will need 10–14 days to cure properly.

A DOG'S LIFE

Hair loss in dogs can have several causes. Seasonal changes in spring may cause dogs to shed hair, which usually grows back in fall or winter. Hormonal replacements may help. Allergies can result in hair loss, too. If shots don't treat the problem, you should test your dog for allergies to food.

A FRIENDLY BONE TO PICK

The thick, wrinkled skin of bulldogs can cause problems. The folds of skin on the face may become infected. If infection is in the face, medicated pads will help. For more widespread infection, special shampoo can treat the problem. Allergies may worsen infection. If your dog doesn't respond to medication and other treatments, the folds may have to be removed surgically.

DOG TALES

■ Bulldogs originally were used in an activity called bull baiting, which was banned in the 1800s. At that time, the dogs were tall, lean, and ferocious.

■ Breeding brought about the physical traits that distinguish bulldogs today and the gentleness that make these dogs great pets.

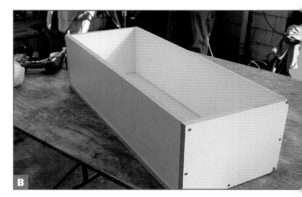

2 Lay the 13½ x 36 bottom piece flat onto a work surface, and take the two other 36" pieces and put them on either edge of the bottom piece. Use the two smaller pieces for the ends of the mold. To attach the smaller pieces, pre-drill ⅛" holes all along the edges where two pieces intersect, and then attach them with 2" wood screws. You should have a mold at 36" long and 10½" high (photo B).

3 Seal the inside seams of the mold with silicone sealant. Place a bead of sealant along all the seams, and smooth out the bead with your finger or a sealant-cornering tool. Go over it a few times to remove the excess sealant. Be sure the seams are as smooth as possible.

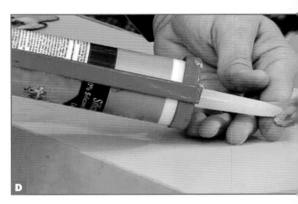

4 The interior mold for the trough is made from a block of polystyrene foam. Shape the foam into a rectangle 33 x 11. You can do this yourself with a hacksaw blade or get it done by your local foam dealer (usually at minimal extra cost).

5 Cover the foam mold with ⅛"-thick PVC sheeting. With a circular saw, cut the sheeting to fit over the foam mold (photo C). Make sure the PVC fits tightly at the seams, and use silicone to adhere it to the foam.

6 Before you place the foam and PVC mold into the wooden mold, you can add decorations that will be inset into the concrete of the finished trough. It is best to use metal (aluminum, stainless steel, etc.) when you add items to the concrete. Use silicone to stick the decorations in the mold, either on the center mold or on the walls of the wooden mold (photo D). The pieces you add should have a protruding part that the concrete can harden around to keep it in place (photo E). Use as many pieces as you want.

7 Place the foam and PVC mold centered into the wooden mold (photo F). Make sure to leave equal distances from one side to the other all the way around. The distance will be the thickness of the trough's walls, and the thicker the better.

8 Mix the concrete with one part hydraulic cement, two parts sand and three parts pea gravel. It's best to use a cement mixer, which is available at your local equipment rental facility. Mix the ingredients in the mixer, and add water until you get a soupy mixture. Dyes are available for concrete, so don't settle for plain gray. We used blue dye, and it looks great.

9 Pour the concrete into the mold slowly to make sure you don't create air pockets. Fill the mold to the top. With a concrete vibrator, vibrate the mixture to release air bubbles that might have been trapped as you poured (Photo G). The concrete vibrator is available at an equipment rental business.

10 Once the concrete is in the mold, it's best for it to cure for 10 to 14 days. That will create a solid trough that should last for a long time. If you are in a rush, you can open the mold in as little as three days, but be careful when you remove the molds because the concrete won't be at its hardest state.

11 To remove the molds from the trough, remove the screws from the wooden outer mold, and slowly and carefully pry off the pieces (photo H). Turn over the trough, and remove the foam from the inner mold. There's no need to be careful with the foam, so break it away from the PVC sheet that covered it (photo I). The PVC should peel away from the concrete easily and leave you with a finished trough.

12 Add a drainpipe to the trough at one end at the bottom center of the wall (photo J). Use a hammer drill with a 34" drill bit to make the hole. Insert an 8"-long piece of ½" copper pipe into the hole, and keep one  end flush with the inner wall of the trough (photo K). Fill the gap in the hole with silicone sealant. Use a rubber stopper to plug the pipe.

13 You may add a manufactured automatic waterer to the trough to give your dog fresh water all year. It's best to drain the water in the trough every three to five days, depending on how many dogs you have, so the water is fresh.

CANINE SUPPLY CABINET

This is a great answer to a storage problem for pet supplies. And if your kitchen doesn't have much counter space, you'll gain surface work area, too. The cabinet holds two kinds of food and has a special place for treats, medications, and leashes.

◀ **PROJECT SUMMARY** ▶

This cabinet is a basic box made from shop-grade plywood. It will have two doors, one of which will be attached to a pullout mechanism that will hold different kinds of dog food. The other door will be mounted on hinges to give more room for supplies.

CANINE SUPPLY CABINET
STEP BY STEP

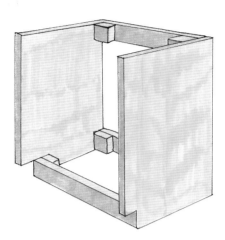

You Will Need

- 1 sheet of ½" plywood, 4 x 8
- A 2 x 4, 6' long
- Store-bought drawer-glide system
- ⅜" offset hinges
- 2 angle brackets
- Safety glasses
- Tape measure
- Pencil
- Table saw
- Circular saw
- Electric drill
- Jigsaw
- 2" wood screws
- Wood glue
- Wood putty
- Putty knife
- Sandpaper
- Paint
- Paintbrush
- Round-over bit
- Router

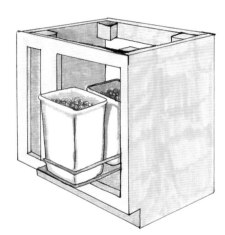

1 Mark a single piece of 4 x 8 plywood ¾" thick as follows:

- Walls, 2 pieces 23 x 34½ with a notch 4" high by 3" deep
- Face frame, 28 x 31
- Floor, 26½ x 23
- Toe kick, 4 x 23
- Back stretcher, 4 x 23
- Top back stretcher, 5 x 23
- Big door, 23¾ x 16¾
- Hinged door, 23¾ x 6¾

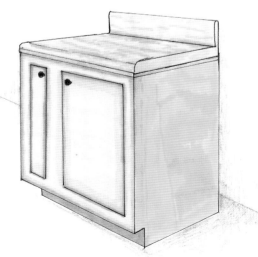

CHOW TIME

DESIGN DECISIONS

The cabinet serves several needs. It provides a place to store your dog's food and treats, pet supplies and medication. And the cabinet top offers more work space. The 16" door is attached to a pullout mechanism that holds two kinds of food. A 6" door mounted on hinges gives more storage space for supplies.

MAKING A HOUSE A HOME

Building tips: By cutting everything from a single sheet of 4 x 8 shop-grade birch plywood, you'll cut your materials cost about in half.

Estimated building time: 6-8 hours

A DOG'S LIFE

Digestive problems can be caused by dietary troubles, parasites or allergies. If your dog has allergies, a hypoallergenic diet can help calm the stomach and intestines.

A FRIENDLY BONE TO PICK

It may be hard to see your dog if you exercise him at night. Some devices help illuminate your pooch. A tag clipped on the collar has a light that flashes when the dog walks. And a headlamp worn around the dog's neck acts as a flashlight.

DOG TALES

▬ Greyhounds, with a lifespan of about 13 years, are 25" to 29" tall and weigh 55 to 60 pounds. Their slim build belies that most are couch potatoes.

▬ Spinones are Italian pointers. They live about 12 years, weigh 60 to 65 pounds and are 22½" to 27½" tall. These strong dogs are bred for hunting.

▬ Terriers, which range from small to very large, are feisty and energetic. They like to dig, chew and bark, and may run away, so it's good to have them in a fenced yard.

2 Cut out all the components with the table saw and circular saw (photo A).

3 Mark openings on the face frame for the doors 23 x 16 and 23 x 6. Leave 2½" at the bottom of the face frame for both doors, and make sure there are at least 2" between the doors. Drill pilot holes in the corners, and use a jigsaw to cut out the door openings (photo B).

4 Cut 10 cleats 4" long from a piece of 1½ x 1½ wood.

5 Attach the cleats to the inside of the side walls at the toe kick and back stretcher rail locations with the 2" wood screws and wood glue. Attach the toe kick and stretcher rails to the side walls by drilling them into the cleats (photo C). Then cleat and attach the floor.

6 Attach the cleats along the vertical front inside lengths of the side walls (photo D). Place the face frame, and drill through the frame into the cleats (photo E).

7 Use the wood putty to fill all the holes left by the screws. After the putty dries, sand it to make it smooth. Paint the entire structure.

CHOW TIME

There are many unconventional diets out there, and one of the most talked about is the bones and raw food, or B.A.R.F diet. A bones and raw food diet is made up primarily of uncooked meat which can lead to many problems. In about 80 percent of the samples tested from commercial and homemade preparations of this diet, there was salmonella in the food. In fact, about 30 percent of the dogs that eat this diet become salmonella carriers. Another problem with the diet is the bones. You can crush the bones up so they do not cause a choking hazard to your dog, but they can still lead to constipation. If you're considering using some sort of bones and raw food diet, the best thing to do is supplement the commercial food your dog is eating with fruits and vegetables. Make sure you wash off the chemicals before you use them, and limit the percentage to 10 to 20 percent of what your dog is eating.

▪ When buying commercial food, dry food is generally better than the wet variety for dogs. Canned foods are good for dogs that don't take in a lot of water.

▪ The different shapes of kibble are made to please the human eye. They don't affect the quality of the food.

▪ Changing brands of foods from time to time is a good idea to ensure a healthy, well balanced diet.

8 To finish the doors, use the round-over router bit to route the round-over along the outside perimeter of both doors. Flip both doors over, and make a ⅜ x ⅜ rabbit cut around the perimeter of each door with the router (photo F).

9 Shim up 1" from the floor of the cabinet to allow clearance for the drawer glides. Install a store-bought drawer-glide system to the shims in the cabinet (photo G).

TIPS | DIY Network Home Improvement

WHAT IS A RABBET?
Sure, it sounds like an animal that your dog would love to get his paws on. But for woodworkers, a rabbet is a groove cut along or near the edge of a piece of wood. Although they are often used to make joints, rabbets have other uses, such as creating grooves on the inside of a cabinet door to help recess it into the face frame.

10 Mark and attach the door using the screws provided with the unit. Attach the storage units to the right-side wall with a level to make sure they are even. Attach the small door with ⅜" offset hinges.

11 Install the cabinet, and attach it to the wall using the angle brackets (photo H). Then attach the countertop by screwing it to the cabinet from underneath.

H

BASIC BUILDING TOOLS

To complete the projects in this book or projects of your own design, you must have the right tools. This section contains an extensive, defined listing of tools for your ideal workshop. Understanding each tool's capabilities is valuable for woodworkers and hobbyists of every experience level. Not all of the tools listed are necessary, but it's a good investment to build a collection of tools needed for most jobs.

An experienced woodworker will recognize that power tools considerably speed up the work process, which will be valuable for a professional. However, a hobbyist should have the freedom to work at his/her own pace and may prefer hand tools. Still, much is to be gained from power tools, which are highly accurate and require less energy to operate than hand tools.

◀ MEASURING AND MARKING TOOLS ▶

The most important step in construction is in the planning, measuring and marking of lengths, joints, and angles. Measuring tools measure length, width and depth. You'll need them at the lumberyard when double-checking stock dimensions, and then back at your workshop when you're building your project. Use your marking tools to designate the lines, points, curves and angles where you must cut or rout.

Steel Tape Measure. Measuring tapes come in lengths of 6' to 25' or more and between ¼" and 1" wide. They are long, bendable rulers which roll up into compact cases. The tape can attach to a work being measured by a hook on one end. It should be loosely mounted to compensate for the width of the hook in measurements. Every ¹⁄₁₆" graduation is noted (and ¹⁄₃₂" increments for the first foot). Our favorite steel tape measure is a ¾" wide, 16' long, self-retracting ruler with a tape-lock button.

Straightedge. When drawing straight lines across short distances, you can't go wrong with a straightedge. A straightedge is basically a steel or aluminum ruler, 12" to 36" long. When graduated clearly, the straightedge can be used for fine measuring and marking.

Combination Square. The combination square is a 4½" x 12" adjustable tool with a sliding blade and a 45-degree built-in shoulder. At any point, the blade can be locked and its end used for measuring and marking.

Try Square. Check or "try" right angles with this square; the ruler along its edges also comes in handy, as do the 6- to 12"-long blades.

Framing Square. Shaped like a large right angle, a framing square is used mainly in construction carpentry to check for 90-degree accuracy on a large scale. Its two edges are 16" x 24" long, and ruler graduations are marked in ⅛" and ⅟₁₆" increments.

Scratch Awl. With a scratch awl, you can mark the starting point for a drill bit, or use a sharpened awl to score a line for marking or cutting. The awl is simply a steel point several inches long with a rounded handle. The scribe is a refined version of the scratch awl.

Marking Gauge. Use a marking gauge to scribe a line at a point in relation to an edge. The gauge is a graduated inch-scale beam which can be centered in hardwood stock. A thumbscrew locks the beam in position, and a steel spur at the end marks the wood when the gauge is pushed along the work.

Compass. A compass is used to record and transfer radius arcs, circles, and patterns during the layout process. It has a pivot at the top and two legs, one with a pointed end and one with a pencil tip.

Protractor. A woodworker's protractor simply determines angles. It has a head with a flat base, upon which a pivoting ruler is attached. The ruler is aligned with the angle, which is then indicated in degrees on a graduated scale etched into the head.

Level. A level establishes whether a framing member is level (if it's horizontal) or plumb (if it's vertical). A bubble captured within a small tube of liquid determines the degree off of center the object in question may be. For accurate work, a level of at least 2' in length is needed. The level itself consists of a long, thin frame of aluminum or wood holding three bubble vials, two at the end positioned to read for plumb, and one in the center set to read for level.

◣ PLANING TOOLS ◢

When buying wood, you will find some of it may be rough-cut or surfaced (planed) on one or two sides only. It's up to you to do the rest, to custom-size your own stock, unless you have a woodshop do it for you. Planes are used to bring the thickness of the wood to a uniform level.

Bench Plane. The edge of this hand-held tool's blade, set within a steel frame, is adjusted to protrude slightly from a slot in the sole, or base, of the body. Hand planes are sold in many varieties, but start with a 1¾" to 2" blade and a sole 9" to 10" long.

Other planes, such as the block plane, are used to make the projects in the book. A small hand-sized plane, the block plane has a 2" x 6" body and is used for detail work.

Power Plane. A hand-held power tool used to plane large amounts of stock from a board's surface quickly, a typical power plane has a two-edged rotary blade about 3¼" wide and a sole between 10" and 12" long. A power plane can remove from ⅟₃₂" to ⅟₁₆" of wood in each pass, depending on its horsepower and the speed of its rotary cutter.

Thickness Planer. A thickness planer is a stationary tool used to plane rough-cut boards to a uniform thickness. Relatively inexpensive, a portable or bench-top planer can handle boards up to 12" wide and 6" thick, removing a maximum of ⅟₁₆" of material with each pass. A larger, standing stationary planer costs three to six times more, and can accommodate a board up to 20" wide and 8" thick. Higher-amperage or 220-volt service may be needed for these larger tools.

Jointer. A jointer is a large standing tool designed to level the face of a board and put a consistent and accurate edge on it in preparation for making a joint. A saw blade by itself cannot make a perfectly accurate cut because there's no true reference on a warped board to work from.

Most jointers are stand-mounted and built to handle boards to 6" to 8" wide, though benchtop jointers do exist. In order to cut beveled edges, a large fence was designed to tilt 45 degrees right and left. The truly competitive jointers cut to ½" depth and can complete a ½" rabbet.

CUTTING TOOLS

The number, pitch, bevel, and angle of teeth on its blade determine the function of a saw. The more teeth per inch of blade, or points, the smoother the blade's cut will be. A saw with fewer points will make a coarser cut, but it will also cut more quickly. A backsaw, for instance, with 15 teeth per inch, is adept for fine joinery work; a crosscut saw, given 8 teeth per inch, can tear quickly through thick lumber. Power saws often use combination blades, which cleanly cut both with and against the wood's grain. Various other blades are made to cut other sheet products.

Crosscut Saw. Cut across or against the wood's grain with a crosscut saw. A 26" version will accommodate most of the hand-sawing in this book—with the exception of plywood, though crosscut saw lengths do vary. Crosscut saw teeth vary from 7 to 12 points per inch, depending on how fine of a cut you desire. Remember, the greater the number of points, the smoother and slower the cut will be made.

Ripsaw. Cut with or along the wood's grain with a ripsaw. Most run 26" long and have 4½ to 7 points per inch. If you prefer to use hand tools, you'll need both a ripsaw and crosscut saw because while it is possible to rip with a crosscut saw, you can't make a crosscut with a ripsaw.

Backsaw. A backsaw is a fine-toothed handsaw, and therefore used in joinery to make smooth, accurate cuts. The saw gets its name from the steel back frame fastened to the uppermost edge of the blade.

Backsaws run 4" to 14" in length, and depending on their purpose, they are classified as thumb, gentleman's, and tenon saws.

Coping Saw. A very thin blade, with 10 to 12 teeth per inch, is mounted between the tips of the coping saw's U-shaped steel-bow frame. Cutting curves is a specialty of the coping saw because its frame can be angled away from the line of cut. Typically it cuts boards thinner than ¾".

Miter Box. A miter box is a wooden or metal frame used in conjunction with a backsaw to handcut miters in boards and trim. Beveled miter cuts can be made as well with specially designed compound miter boxes.

Circular Saw. A hand-held, motor-driven saw, the circular saw has a 7¼" blade that's adjustable to angled cuts. The blade penetration varies by degree, from 2¼" at 90 degrees to 1¾" at 45 degrees. Unfortunately, the size and weight of the circular saw negatively affect its accuracy. Be on the lookout for circular saws with carbide-tipped combination blades, though regular, less expensive blades are fine if you clean or replace them regularly. An excellent blade can upgrade the performance of an inexpensive saw.

Compound Miter Saw. A portable power saw that's evolved in several versions, the compound miter saw is also known as a chop saw or cutoff saw. Similar to a circular saw, the least expensive version pulls down to cut and swings from left to right to cut miters. Unlike the circular saw, it's mounted on a short table with a pivoting hinge. A beveling feature that tilts the blade as well for a compound level cut is included in the next level. Our pick is the model with a slide mount so the blade and motor move up and down up to 1' like a radial-arm saw, and it cuts miters and bevels as well. Blade diameters run from 8½" to 12".

Radial-Arm Saw. Radial-arm saws are stationary power saws used to cross-cut long pieces of wood on a large fixed table. It's a versatile saw with a powerful motor and a 10" blade suspended on a carriage from a beam which can be swung right and left and raised and lowered as well. The saw can also make bevel cuts, and a pivot in the carriage allows the motor and blade to be turned 90 degrees for making rip cuts as well.

Table Saw and Dado Blade. Built into a frame and table, the table saw uses a heavy motor. The table saw's weight and design cuts more accurately than a hand-held circular saw. The blade is raised to a 90-degree cutting depth of $3\frac{1}{8}$" (or at 45 degrees, a cutting depth of $2\frac{1}{8}$").

A pivoting carriage holds the blade's arbor or axle. Table saws are generally equipped with a 10" carbide-tipped combination blade. Smaller bladed models carry the same features as the larger models. The long, straight bar that runs parallel to the exposed blade and can be adjusted to either side of it is called the rip fence. It ensures that material is being guided to the blade for accurate rip cuts.

A miter gauge helps in making miter cuts. It's adjustable to 45 degrees on either side of its 90-degree midpoint and holds the wood in place at the correct angle as it's being passed through the blade.

Fitted to a table saw, a dado blade is especially designed to make wide grooves and notches. There are two common dado designs: an offset blade that wobbles to the right and to the left as it revolves, and two outer blades and a number of inner "chippers" that are stacked side by side to establish the exact width of the cut.

Jigsaw. A powered alternative to the coping saw, the jigsaw is used for cutting curves, free-form shapes, and large holes in panels or boards up to $1\frac{1}{2}$" thick. It is sometimes called the Saber saw. Cutting action is provided by a narrow blade which moves very rapidly. A shoe surrounding the blade can be tilted 45 degrees for angled cuts. The best jigsaws have variable speed control and orbital blade action—meaning the cutting edge is swung forward into the work and back again, through the blade's up-and-down cycle. The jigsaw also comes with a dust blower to keep the cut clear, a circle-cutting guide, and a rip fence.

Utility Knife. This tool can cut thin wood and material, and mark lines for measuring. Look for utility knives with two or three blade positions, including a fully retractable one.

CLAMPING TOOLS

Clamps are quite useful—they hold parts to each other to the bench so you can mark, drill, or cut them, and they're also great for holding glued parts together while the glue dries. Clamps also function as saw and route guides when used with strips of wood or can be extended to clamp over a large area.

C-Clamps. C-clamps are named after the basic C shape of their steel frames. The anvil end of the C is fixed—it doesn't move at all, while the other end, fitted with a threaded rod and swivel panel, is tightened so that whatever it contains is tightly gripped. Use scrap pieces of pads as a buffer so that your work isn't harmed when the clamp is tightened. C-clamps are generally small, though they come in a variety of styles and sizes; woodworking C-clamps are usually limited to a 12" jaw opening, but for the projects in this book, a 4" or 6" size is fine.

Bar and Pipe Clamps. Unlike C-clamps, bar and pipe clamps can hold great expanses of material, like panels or doors, or grip several pieces of wood edged together. Several feet of steel, aluminum, or iron bars or piping make up the clamps. A fixed head, equipped with a short, threaded rod and a metal pad, is at one end, and at the other is a sliding tail stop lockable in any position along the bar or pipe. Pipe clamps are the less expensive option of the two, and they are also more flexible than bar clamps and can be made in excess of 6'. You can purchase pipe clamp kits with the fixtures and be set to go with a bit of help in threading the pipe from your local plumbing supply store.

Vises. A bench-mounted clamp is a vise. It can be used to hold stock securely when you work on it or to hold work pieces together. Better wood vises include a dog—a bar that slides up from the vise's movable jaw to hold work against a similar stop mounted on the bench itself. The dog extends the vise's effective jaw opening by 2' or more. Some vises also use a half-nut to provide quick-slide opening and closing; tightening occurs only once the work is in place. It's important the vise has smooth, broad jaws that are drilled so that facings can be installed to prevent harming fine work.

◀ DRILLING AND BORING TOOLS ▶

Drills and bits are necessary for cutting clean holes through wood. Try drilling functional holes or holes with special features like tapered countersink openings or an open shoulder.

⅜" Variable-Speed Reversible Drill. It's possible to bore any drill with a hand drill, but why waste time and effort when this power drill does the job more quickly and easily. For most any project, a drill with a ⅜" chuck capacity and a motor amperage of 3.5 amps or greater will do just fine. Cordless versions are good for driving screws and drilling small holes, but they may not be suitable for continuous, heavy-duty work.

An electric drill with a variable-speed control is worth the small extra cost. Variable-speed control means the drill's motor is connected to the pressure you exert on the tool's trigger. A reversible motor, included with this model, enables you to take screws out as quickly as you inserted them.

Stop Collars. Stop collars are metal (or sometimes plastic) rings that tighten onto the drill bit's shaft.

They are sized to fit different drill-bit diameters and are used to control the depth of a drill bit's penetration. The collar hits the wood's face and stops the bit from going any deeper.

Countersinks. There's nothing more unsightly than a protruding screw above the face of wood. Countersinks are used to hide these heads. They fit into the surface of the work by cutting shallow, slope-side holes into which the screw's head rests, flush with the face of the work.

Brace and Bit. A brace is a two-handed drill that operates like a crank—it's most helpful for drilling deep or large-diameter holes cleanly and accurately. At the top of the drill is a handle that allows the rank to pivot and keeps it in line. A two-jawed chuck grips a spiral boring bit, or some type of expansion bit at the lower end. The working hand turns the grip on the crank to slowly bore the opening.

Specialty Bits. There is a variety of drill bits tailored to accomplish specific tasks. For example, use a Forstner bit to drill clean, finely cut flat-bottomed holes. They are made in ¼" to 2¼" diameters. Another bit, the spade bit, is used with power drills to quickly bore and make rough but effective holes through wood. They're designed with a center point and two flat cutting edges and come in ¼" to 1½" diameters.

To bore holes deeper than a normal-length bit would allow, use extension bits or extension shafts over spade bits. The extra-length bits come in diameters from ³⁄₁₆" to ¾" and usually are 18" long; the spade bit extension shafts come in 18" and 24" lengths and are made to fit standard ⁵⁄₁₆" and ⁷⁄₁₆" power-bit shanks.

To combine the hole-drilling and countersinking processes, use screw bits. Tapered bits, an improvement on the basic screw bits, follow the contour of a standard wood screw; they also include a stop collar. These combination bits are made for screw size Nos. 5 through 12. Versatility is the emphasis of screw bits: not only can you countersink a fastener flush with the wood's surface, but you can also counter-bore a deeper hole.

CHISELING AND ROUTING TOOLS

To achieve fine joinery and decorate work, you must have tools able to make sharp, detailed cuts or create a consistent design along the face of a piece of wood. Both power- and hand-operated tools work fine; what matters is the sharpness of the tool's cutting edge.

Chisels. Most projects require the standard mortise chisel. It's a cabinetmaker's tool used to clean up joints and mortises, shave glue and grain from a joint, or simply remove layers of wood from one spot. Try a set of four or five bevel-edge chisels for hand or mallet work, in sizes from ¼" to 1" wide.

Routers. A router does many things—it cuts grooves and rabbets, shapes edges and makes slots, all quickly and easily. Rounded or chamfered edges can be cut with a router and a roundover or chamfer bit. You can try to do the same work with gouges, rasps or sanders, but it comes out looking inconsistent.

Router bits are held in a collet on the end of a shaft, which in turn is supported by a flat base and housing. The bit's shape determines what type of cut will be made in the work. Handles on the housing give the operator control of the direction of the bit.

The simplest routers have ⅜" collets, external clamp-depth controls, and low-amperage motors. More sophisticated models are known as plunge routers; these allow vertical entry into the work for precise cutting and have ½" collets, variable-speed 12- to 15-amp motors, and variable-depth controls.

For best results, use the router on a routing table—a stand with a cast surface that uses a heavy-duty ½" router inverted and mounted from the bottom. An adjustable fence and a special see-through guard allow you to guide the work through the exposed bit safely.

A stationary routing tool, a shaper uses a powerful motor and ½" or ¾" spindle to do heavier work than a table-mounted router, such as moldings, heavy raised panels, and hardwood trim.

Router Bits. Note the design and shape of a router bit, as it is reflected in the finished project's edges or grooves. Over 200 router-bit styles are available for various types of work, but for the projects in this book, only a few will be needed. A router bit with a ball-bearing pilot at its tip is used when cutting or shaping an edge—the tip rolls along the edge below the part of the wood being cut, ensuring a high degree of accuracy.

A guide or temporary fence is often used when routing a channel, as groove- or slot-cutting bits cannot use pilot tips. A guide is a device that clamps onto the base of the tool and acts as a moving fence for the router and bit to follow the edge of the work. Set the bit vertically by adjusting the router base to control the depth of cut.

JOINING TOOLS

Now that the boards and components are ready for joining, several tools can be used to complete the joint. You can take the traditional road with back-saws and chisels, or try newer methods.

Doweling Jig. Mainly used for edge-joining and certain framing applications, the doweling jig is a precision frame used to center holes on the edge of a board up to about 2" thick. To correspond with the dowel sizes being used, various-sized holes are on the jig in matching places, so the edges of the joined boards are aligned both vertically and horizontally.

Biscuit Joiners. A high-speed rotary saw with a blade about 4⅛" in diameter and 4 mm thick, the biscuit joiner is also known as the plate joiner. The cutter slices the work horizontally because it is placed on the vertical axis. An adjustable miter fence allows joinery on square and beveled edges. A depth adjuster sets the plunge level to correspond with the size of biscuit being used. Three different sizes of biscuits are available (Nos. 0, 10, and 20), and they range in length from $2\frac{1}{8}$" to $2\frac{9}{16}$" and in width from $1\frac{1}{8}$"to $1\frac{7}{8}$".

HAMMERING AND SETTING TOOLS

Hammers. You'll probably use a lightweight, $3\frac{1}{2}$ to 6 ounce tack hammer to do most finishing work.

Nail set. To set the head of a finishing nail or brad below the surface of the wood without enlarging the hole, a nail set is used.

Mallets. An 8" wooden carpenter's mallet of 12 ounces or so does the work of a larger hammer on chisel work or setting joints. A plastic-headed hammer also works.

Screwdriving Tools. Throughout this book, screw fasteners have a No. 2 Phillips head to give a positive and usually slipless grip. Drive larger Phillips-head screws (No. 12 and up) with a No. 3 Phillips screwdriver tip.

Screwdrivers. A 6" or 8" No. 2 Phillips driver with a molded or wooden handle is the one to use on the No. 6, No. 8 and No. 10 Phillips-head screws usually used in this book's projects. If you choose to use traditional slotted screws, a $\frac{3}{16}$" and $\frac{1}{4}$" straight blade are needed. Square-drive screw heads naturally use square-tip drivers.

Power Drivers. To save time, most woodworkers use power-drive bits in combination with cabinet or drywall screws. Often used with hand-held drivers or $\frac{3}{8}$" variable-speed power drills, these bits have a short, six-sided shank which slips easily into the drill chuck. Use a tip that's a Phillips or straight-bladed design or a square-drive tip to fit matching screws.

SANDING AND SMOOTHING TOOLS

Before finishing a piece, sanding and smoothing has to be done to level surfaces. Files and rasps cut or round edges and small areas whereas sandpaper prepares the wood for its final finish.

Rasps and Files. Used to make the first cut in removing wood stock for shaping or rounding, wood rasps are coarse-cutting hand tools. A finer cabinet rasp is made for the second round of cutting. Choose from three styles of rasps: flat on both sides, half-round on one side, and round.

Less coarse than rasps, wood files are used for finer smoothing and finishing work. Wood files are about the same size as rasps—10" long, and they usually come in round and half-round cross sections. Only a flat rasp may be needed for this book's projects. It's a good idea to have two grades of files on hand—a 10" or 12" bastard-cut file and a smooth-cut file. The bastard-cut file is one step finer than a coarse file, with a half-round back which allows it to be used on inside curves and arcs. The smooth-cut file, the least course of the group, is used for finish work and is especially suited to hardwoods.

Sanders and Sandpaper. Sand by hand or with power sanders. Purchase a hand-sanding block if you choose to sand by hand. The hand-held orbital finishing sander—called a palm or pad sander—has a palm or square pad to which sandpaper is attached. The orbiting mechanism uses a 2-amp motor. The round styles use self-adhesive paper on the pad rather than mechanical clips.

BASIC BUILDING TECHNIQUES

This section is designed for newcomers to woodworking. Beginner builders can get comfortable with the terminology and pick up new techniques by carefully reviewing this section. Experienced woodworkers will find this chapter worthy of review, too—it's a chance to refresh your memory of basic skills and terminology.

The preliminary measuring and marking stage is as important as buying the right tools. It's all about how you use the tools: you shouldn't rely on a tape measure to make a straight line or a square blade to make a circle. It's also important to stick with the same tools throughout the completion of the project—switching tapes or marking gauges in midstream is the cause of many small mistakes.

Most general measuring begins with the steel tape because it's fast and accurate within $1/16"$—acceptable for almost any but the finest of woodworking projects. A steel tape has its limitations, though. For example, it can't mark a straight line over any distance: the metal band will move or distort no matter how careful you are. For distances less than 3', rely on a straightedge for marking a straight line.

For a greater distance, try a chalk line—a chalking string stretched between two points—or you can use the steel tape to mark short increments over a greater distance, then strike lines between them with a straightedge if need be.

For marking for a cut, most woodworkers use a steel scribe or a pointed awl trip. However, a sharp pencil can be used to make a very accurate V-shaped mark, pointing to the cutting site.

Use a square to mark a square, perpendicular edge, crosscuts, or transfer a line to the remaining three sides of a board. For smaller jobs, use a try square, and for larger projects, use a framing square. Lay the stock, or handle, of the tool against the edge of the work and mark a line, in pencil, along the blade. For transferring the line to the side and back surfaces, walk the square around the work, using the tail of the previous line as the start of the next one, and so on.

Use a compass for laying out a radius of partial or full circles. Open its legs to the correct radius, then place the point at the center of the circle or arc you wish to make and swing the other leg to make the mark. A radius is half a circle's width, or diameter. A protractor simplifies measuring angles. Either the standard transparent protractor or the stainless steel kind with degree-graduations along the edge is fine. Match the bottom of the protractor with the work's baseline. Read the measurement at the top arc. A more sophisticated bevel protractor has a pivoting arm that makes it easier to read or establish the existing angle or bevel.

Establish the degree off of "plumb" (straight up-and-down) or "level" (horizontally straight) of a framing member with a level. Lay the level's frame against the side or top of the framing member. Watch the bubble in the appropriate vial—for plumb measurement, use the end vials; use the center vial for determining level—to see how true the piece is. Remember, a centered bubble is perfectly accurate.

◢ CUTTING STRAIGHTS AND CURVES ◣

After the measuring and marking, making the cuts is a matter of following the lines. Remember to double-check your measuring work: measure twice, cut once.

To rip, saw with the grain of the wood. Rip handsaws firmly, but not tensely, with the back of the handle squarely against the ball of your palm. Use the outer edge of your thumb to guide the teeth when starting a cut. The cut should be made on the waste, or outer side, of the line. Begin the cut on the upstroke; the sides of the blade must be squared with the surface of the wood.

For crosscuts, hold tools at a 45-degree angle; with rip cuts, work at 60 degrees. Deliver the cutting pressure only on the downstroke.

When using a circular saw, make sure the teeth fully penetrate the opposite face of the work by setting the blade depth—adjust it by loosening a knob and moving the shoe up or down. This will clear sawdust particles and make the blades less likely to jam. Also, be careful not to cut your sawhorse or workbench.

Carefully set yourself in a comfortable position before using the saw, but remember not to lean too far forward, otherwise you'll end up off balance at the end of a long cut. Be careful not to grip the handle too tightly either—it'll tire your hands and possibly create inaccuracies in your work. Some larger saws come with a second grip; however, remember that clamping is required with two-handed saws.

Remember to always wear safety glasses when using any saw. Watch the power cord; be sure to draw it behind you before starting the tool. Sight your line of cut along the reference mark on the front of the saw's shoe. The safety guard swings up by itself as you progress with the saw.

A table saw cuts more accurately than a circular saw thanks to its guide fence and miter gauge. A handwheel located at the front of the saw cabinet sets the cutting depth; judge the depth of cut by watching the blade—several full teeth should be exposed during the cut, which cools the blade and allows sawdust to escape.

Loosen the lock and slide the fence to the right or left as needed to adjust the fence. To measure the width of the cut, use the gauge on the fence rails, or for greater accuracy, take a steel-tape reading between the fence's edge and the tip of a blade tooth set toward the fence.

Once you start the motor, give it a few seconds to come up to speed; never shove a piece of wood into a slowly moving blade. Don't ever put your hands near the spinning blade; use a push stick about 18" in length to pass the work through.

The basic curve-cutting tool for thinner material and very taut contours is a thin-bladed coping saw because it's easily controlled. For stock more than $3/8$" thick, or a line greater than the throat depth of the saw, use a handheld electric jigsaw. Tighter curves or circles require thinner jigsaw blades so that the jigsaw doesn't bind or overheat.

There are several ways to cut at an angle, just as there are several ways to make miters and bevels. Miters are angle-cuts made across the face of a board, for example, the corners of a picture frame; bevels are angle cuts into the edge of a board, as in a piece of trim or molding. Finally, a compound cut is a combination of miters and beveling. For wood less than 6" wide, use a miter box with a fine backsaw for the most accurate miter cut.

For bevel cutting, adjust the shoe on a circular saw to a 45-degree angle. For even greater accuracy, adjust the table saw blade to the same angle by using the handwheel on the side of the cabinet.

For mitering with a table saw, loosen the knob on the miter gauge and adjust its fence to the desired angle, then tighten the knob. Hold the work against the fence, so that the gauge and the work move forward to meet the blade.

Cut a rabbet or groove with a table saw fitted with a dado blade, or use a router and straight bit. Remember that when using the table saw you must remove the table insert and dado blade width.

There are two ways to do this, depending on the blade design. The width of an offset "wobler" blade is changed by a rotating hub, while a stacked type must be set out of the saw and reinstalled on the arbor. Make sure that the teeth rest between the gullets of the adjacent blades and that the chippers are staggered around the circumference when you stack the chippers between the outer blades.

The handwheel adjusts the depth of the blade and sets the fence to establish the position of the rabbet or groove on the work. Be careful not to cut too quickly as the blade has a lot to do cutting that much wood at once.

◄ GROOVING AND JOINING ►

Clean and straightened surfaces that haven't been fully cut with a saw or drill are required for mortises and mortised hinges. This is accomplished with a chisel, which is fairly easy to do as long as the chisel has a consistently sharp edge.

A mallet isn't necessary for most work; push the work by holding the chisel in your right hand while using your left hand to guide the blade's direction. Mallet users should strike the tool lightly to avoid taking big bites at once. Hold the tool at a slight right

or left angle whenever possible while working with the grain to ensure smooth cuts that are less likely to dull the blade. Avoid gouging the work by not driving the edge too steeply—hold the blade at a slight downward angle.

A router handles deeper cuts or shaping work quickly and cleanly, while it would take quite some time with a saw and chisel. The finished edge or groove's look is determined by the shape of the router bit's cutting surface. A slot the width of the bit itself is made by a straight bit; a clean, rounded edge is cut into a squared surface by a roundover bit; a beveled edge is cut by a chamfer bit; a detailed profile is cut by an ogee.

Position yourself with two hands loosely gripping the router and a clear view of the working bit when operating a router, and be sure to wear safety goggles. Movement is from left to right, except when circular or irregular cutting, in which case the motion is counter-clockwise. First make cuts across the end grain of your work, then avoid chipping by working with the grain.

Control the depth of cut by loosening the base of the router and adjusting the motor housing up or down. To preview what your work will look like, run a test on a piece of scrap wood before you make any permanent cuts. Your control of the tool will improve with practice, and soon you'll be able to rely on the depth gauge marked on the side of the router rather than having to test every cut you make.

Freehand work is fine for short jobs; however, when making long cuts, you'll need to clamp the wood to a bench and use the tool's base-mounted guide to keep the cut straight. If without a guide, substitute by clamping a straight section of 1 x 2 to the bench or your work parallel to the line you wish to cut.

Place a piece of scrap stock to the right and left of the work, flush with the working surface, to rout narrow stock or edge–rabbet grooves—this prevents the routing guide from tilting to one side and spoiling the cut and gives you a place to mount a guide if you use one.

DRILLING AND COUNTERSINKING

Three parts make up the screw hole: the pilot or lead hole (which is little more than half the diameter of the screw itself), the shank or body hole (the same diameter as the screw), and the sink or bore, used if the screw head is to be recessed below the surface of the wood.

You only need to drill the pilot hole for a short screw in softwoods, though dense hardwoods and long screws sometimes call for a shank hole, too. Remember, make that hole only as deep as the shank—the unthreaded portion of the screw—is long. Also remember that a screw driven perpendicular to the grain has twice the holding power than a screw driven to the wood's end-grain.

Screw bits (countersink and pilot bits) considerably simplify the hole-drilling process. Sized by screw numbers, screw bits have top collars and countersinks adjustable for length. Tapered bits are used to accommodate wood screws perfectly.

When driving into softwoods using $1\frac{1}{2}$" or shorter No. 6 and No. 8 diameters, cabinet screws are even easier to use. These self-tapping, power-driven screws don't need pilot holes, though you should take care to predrill the pilots when working near the end of the wood.

Deck screws, another variation, are coated with a smooth anodization which makes them weather-resistant. They work in both softwoods and hardwoods, though in hardwoods, the screw holes should be predrilled, otherwise you may split the wood or shear the screw head off.

A regular bit can drill socket holes if the diameters are small enough—$\frac{1}{4}$" or $\frac{3}{8}$". For larger holes, you'll need a Forstner bit, which produces a clean, flat-bottomed hole. If you have trouble gauging the depth of a socket correctly, use a stop collar or piece of tape on a standard drill bit.

If another piece is planned to face it, take care when drilling through-holes. In this situation, you can avoid splintering wood by drilling only partially through the piece, then coming at the hole from the opposite side. To locate the point at which you'll start the second hole, use a small pilot bit to penetrate the back face.

CLAMPING

Clamps hold parts together while they're being glued or secure pieces for cutting or drilling. Long and relatively inexpensive for their size, bar or pipe clamps are especially suited for wide clamping jobs. A range of adjustment between the jaws is permitted by a sliding tailpiece.

For joints or pieces less than 12" in depth, choose a C-clamp. Available in standard and deep throat depth, C-clamps all have a threaded rod with a swivel tip that applies pressure to the work as you tighten the rod. Cut 2" square pads from scrap pieces of $\frac{1}{4}$" plywood to prevent the metal tips from marring your work.

Place the clamp's pressure points directly at the centerline of the work or joint to be glued for the best results in joint-clamping. Be careful to snug-tighten, not over-tighten, as over-tightening can damage the wood, and with gluing, squeeze enough adhesive from the joint to cause uneven distribution and a weakened bond.

SANDING AND SMOOTHING

Finishing really depends on the quality of the wood, as well as your technique. With a lot of time and a bit of know-how, you'll perfectly sand or smooth the wood's surface.

Before you get started, take a look at the surface in good light. Before you can safely apply a coating, the wood must be flat with a smooth surface. Check for glue runs or forced material, which should be cleared off before they dry. Otherwise, trim the dried material off with a sharp chisel.

Beware of manufactured wood pieces, especially moldings and trim, which may be contaminated with silicone oils or waxes left there as cutter-head lubricants. Don't fret, they can be removed with a cloth soaked in mineral spirits, followed by an ammonia wash of one part clear ammonia to 15 parts warm water spread evenly over the entire surface then wiped dry. It also depends on the type of your finish: waxes and oils are usually fine with oil-based finishes, but can ruin water-based finishes and lacquers, which is why they must be removed before going any further.

It's time for a quick lesson on sandpaper, or more accurately: coated abrasive. Sandpaper is made of tiny pieces of mineral grit glued onto some kind of backing. Determining how fast a paper will sand, grit also reflects how much effort will be required to sand. Both the backing and the glue, or binder, used to keep the grit in place determine how the grit will stand up to wear and solvents.

Sandpapering is a straightforward process: the abrasive removes tool marks left in the surface of the wood and replaces them with grooves established by the size of the grit on the sandpaper. The errant large grooves are replaced with the sandpaper's many small grooves, especially if a fine grit is used.

"Open coat" and "closed coat" are terms used to describe the amount of grit on the backing. With only 50 percent to 70 percent of the surface covered in mineral, open coat paper provides a place for the cuttings to lodge, and occasionally requires declogging. Completely covered with sand, a closed coat offers a finer finish. Higher-grit (extra-fine) papers don't offer much more because most of the grooves have already been sanded off. To conserve material and make less heat, however, stick with the lower-numbered grits (open style paper).

Grits are made of either synthetic or natural material. Many different materials are available, but only a few apply to wordworking. Of the synthetic grits, you'll probably use aluminum oxide. Light brown or white in color, it's ideal for general sanding and finishing work. If using only one product to finish, use another synthetic, silicon carbide, which is bright black.

Even with the popularity of synthetics, garnet, a reddish mineral, is used often in sandpaper. Breaking off as it works, garnet presents a new sharp facet with each fracture. Though garnet works wonderfully, it does wear faster than synthetics.

Sandpaper backing varies according to the tool it is used with. Both sheet and polyester cloth backings are used, though cloth backings are used more commonly on belt sanders. Hand-held palm sanders commonly have a paper backing with pressure-sensitive adhesive.

Always work from coarse to fine grits when sanding. Begin with an 80 or 100 grit, then progressively increase the point range with each step. A typical progression would be 80/120/220/400.

Choosing grit size is critical. Too heavy a grit usually results in a lot of work with little progress because you're simply creating grooves, while too light a grit doesn't remove the deeper marks created earlier, leaving them in the finish. With softwoods, you usually don't have sand finer than 180 grit. However, the harder words may require a 400-grit or higher. Generally speaking, we recommend a 220-grit sanding for the best results, particularly with a water-based finish.

An alternative to the motor-driven palm sander, a sanding block achieves a flat surface while giving you a better feel for your work. Fold a paper sheet several times to do detail work, or stiffen the paper in your fingers. At the 150-grit level or higher, you may sand in any direction because the scratches will likely be invisible.

When using a palm sander, the most common error is scrubbing it across the wood's surface too quickly. Remember that an oscillating sander already moves at the rate of nearly 14,000 oscillations per minute—you don't need to speed it up. To give you an idea of the ideal speed, your hand (with the sander in it) should move about one inch per second—this should prevent swirl marks from ending up in the finish.

Index

Acknowledgements

The authors would like to thank the following people for the support and creativity they have contributed to the show: Ross Babbit (DIY Network), Bob Baskerville (DIY Network), Preston Farabowk, Ty Crisp, Danny Harb, Scott Minor, Dario Gildrie, David McCauley, Christopher Gurney, Sean Hunt, and Gene Priest.